THE LOVELY BONES

Alice Sebold

AUTHORED by Rachel Younger
UPDATED AND REVISED by Elizabeth Weinbloom

COVER DESIGN by Table XI Partners LLC
COVER PHOTO by Olivia Verma and © 2005 GradeSaver, LLC

BOOK DESIGN by Table XI Partners LLC

Published by GradeSaver LLC, www.gradesaver.com

First published in the United States of America by GradeSaver LLC. 2010

GRADESAVER, the GradeSaver logo and the phrase "Getting you the grade since 1999" are registered trademarks of GradeSaver, LLC

ISBN 978-1-60259-245-2

Printed in the United States of America

For other products and additional information please visit
http://www.gradesaver.com

Table of Contents

Table of Contents

Table of Contents

Biography of Sebold, Alice (1968-)

Alice Sebold was born on September 6, 1968 in Madison, Wisconsin. She grew up in the suburbs of Philadelphia, Pennsylvania and graduated from Great Valley High School in Malvern, PA in 1980. She went on to attend Syracuse University. Near the end of her freshman year, she was raped in a tunnel on her walk home. When she reported the crime to the police, they told her she was "lucky" because another girl had recently been raped and killed in the same tunnel. She would later name her memoir *Lucky* because of this conversation. A few months after the rape, Sebold saw her rapist on the street and reported him. She testified in court and he got the maximum sentence.

Sebold went home to live with her family for the summer between her freshman and sophomore years. She returned to Syracuse in the fall and continued to study writing there and completed her Bachelor's degree in 1984. Sebold tried to write her story a number of times, but each time she was unable to produce a narrative that was satisfactory to her. She later realized that she was trying to write a story that encompassed all rape victims, and thus the product was fuzzy and bland.

Although there are quasi-religious themes in her work, Sebold stated in an interview with *The Guardian* that she is not religious. Her mother was heavily involved in their church up until after Sebold was raped, when the church members' reacted by saying it must have been Sebold's fault.

After graduating from Syracuse University, Sebold went to the University of Houston in Texas, where she studied poetry from 1984 – 1985, and then moved to New York City. There she taught English and worked as a research analyst and in other jobs while she continued to write. She spent ten years in New York. During this time, she claims to have become a competent New Yorker. Sebold also said in an interview with *The Guardian* that she did many things she was not proud of, such as dating men who were heavy drinkers, and three years of recreational use of heroin. Sebold never became addicted and believes she was self-medicating. Her life was transformed by a book called *Trauma and Recovery*, which helped her realize that she still had not recovered from her rape. She began to go to therapy.

At age 33, Sebold moved to California to pursue a master's degree in fine arts at the University of California in Irvine. There she met her husband, Glen David Gold. Sebold also began to write *Lucky*, a memoir of her rape. It started with a ten-page writing assignment for which Sebold wrote forty pages (none of which were used in the finished piece). She had already begun to write *The Lovely Bones*, but she realized she needed to put it on hold while she wrote her own story. Sebold graduated with an MFA from UCI in 1998. *Lucky* was released in 1999. Sebold's second book, *The Lovely Bones*, was published in 2002 when she was 39 years old. The book sold over a million copies and was critically acclaimed across the United States. Sebold's second novel, *The Almost Moon*, was published in 2007 and received mixed reviews.

Sebold lives in California. She told *The Guardian* that she often gets up at 3 AM to write because she likes to write in the dark. Although the topics of her novels are dark, she signs her books "Viva!" emphasizing her belief that people who have experienced violence can go on living, just as she did.

About The Lovely Bones

The Lovely Bones, released in 2002, is Alice Sebold's second published book, and her first published novel. The book sold almost three million copies and was on the *New York Times* bestseller list for over a year. The novel was translated into over forty languages. Before it was published, an excerpt of the book was run in the magazine *Seventeen*. The TV show i[Good Morning America] featured the novel in their book club shortly after it was published. *The Lovely Bones* won the Bram Stoker award for Best First Novel in 2002, and was nominated for Best Novel, both by the Horror Writers Association. *The Lovely Bones* received rave reviews from American critics, including the i[New York Times] critic Kakutani who commented that the novel is a "keenly observed portrait of familial love and how it endures and changes over time" and praised Sebold for her ability to capture so much in her writing. Many other American critics agreed; *Publishers Weekly* called the novel "a story that is both tragic and full of light and grace" and *Booklist* said Sebold "paints, with an artist's precision, a portrait of a world where the terrible and the miraculous can and do co-exist." However, the reviews in Britain were not as full of praise; a number of British critics believed the novel was too sentimental and sweet.

Sebold told i[The Guardian] she writes about violence because she knows many people have experienced it and it is not uncommon. Sebold herself is a rape survivor. Another girl was also raped in the same tunnel where Sebold was attacked, and that girl did not survive - she was murdered and dismembered. While *Lucky* is Sebold's story, some critics have wondered if in *The Lovely Bones* Sebold was trying to write the story of the other girl who was killed in the same tunnel. In *The Guardian* interview, Sebold said that was not her intention, but that the other girl's story could have been subconsciously with her while she was writing. The title of *The Lovely Bones* refers to the relationships that form in the novel after the main character's death.

Sebold's depiction of heaven in the novel is thought by some to be Christian. However, the heaven experienced by Susie does not include God or Jesus. Sebold meant for Susie's heaven to be a simple view of what heaven could be like; Sebold is not religious.

Peter Jackson released a film version of *The Lovely Bones* in January 2010. The film starred Saorise Ronan, Mark Wahlberg, Rachel Weisz, Susan Sarandon and Stanley Tucci. The film received mixed reviews, and was nominated for a number of awards.

Character List

Susie Salmon

The narrator of the story, she is fourteen years old. She is murdered at the beginning of the novel and narrates from heaven. She spends much of her time telling the story of how her family and loved ones cope with her death. Her curiosity also leads her to find out more about her killer. In addition, she narrates her own progression through heaven as she matures there. Although Susie never grows up, her voice is a mix of her adolescent whimsy and her growing maturity acquired in heaven.

George Harvey

The Salmons' neighbor and Susie's murderer. He builds dollhouses for a living. After Susie's death she finds out that Mr. Harvey has murdered a number of girls and women. He always takes a souvenir from each victim. He isolates himself from society and spends much of his time alone.

Lindsey Salmon

Susie's younger sister. She is about 1 year younger than Susie, and is 13 when the novel begins. Lindsey is very athletic and plays soccer, and is considered a gifted student. Susie often lives vicariously through her sister as she grows up. Susie's death forces Lindsey to become more independent and to take on a parenting role in her family. She rarely admits that Susie's death had a profound effect on her, but she thinks of Susie often.

Jack Salmon

Susie, Lindsey and Buckley's father. He is deeply saddened by Susie's death and does everything he can to avenge it. He also feels guilty that he was unable to be there for her when she needed him. While he tries to focus his attention on his two surviving children, he always finds himself thinking of Susie as well.

Abigail Salmon

Susie, Lindsey and Buckley's mother. After Susie's death she distances herself from her family and begins to resent her role as mother. She leaves the family mid-novel in order to pursue her life as an individual and to escape from the pain of Susie's death.

Buckley Salmon

Susie's younger brother. He is four when the novel begins and does not fully understand Susie's death. To add to his confusion, his family hides Susie's death from him in an effort to protect him. Buckley has a close relationship with his father, but he grows up angry and feels that his father loves Susie the most.

Ray Singh

The boy that Susie has a crush on before her death. He gave Susie her first kiss. The Singhs live in the same neighborhood as the Salmons. They are Indian, and Susie found him exotic because he had lived in both India and in London. Susie continues to watch him after her death, and often longs for him.

Len Fenerman

The detective working on Susie's case. He develops a close relationship with the Salmons. He feels guilty that he is unable to solve the case and continues to think of Susie long after the case is closed. he was married once but his wife committed suicide, and he thinks of her as a case that he should be able to solve. He falls in love with Abigail Salmon and they have a brief affair, but Abigail only uses him to forget her pain.

Ruth Connors

As Susie leaves the earth, her soul accidentally touches Ruth. After this experience, Ruth finds out a lot of information about Susie and later invests much of her time in finding places where other women and girls have been killed. Ruth becomes good friends with Ray Singh and they often talk about Susie.

Holiday

The Salmon family dog.

Grandma Lynn

Abigail's mother. She is characterized by her excessive vanity and her frequent drinking. Despite these flaws, Lynn is supportive of the family after Susie's death and helps them cope.

Ruana Singh

Ray Singh's mother. She is characterized by her beauty and her former days as a dancer. She offers support to the Salmons, but she does so in very subtle ways; small conversations and words of advice, her calm manner, and the apple pies she bakes and leaves on their doorstep.

Samuel Heckler

Lindsey's boyfriend, and later her husband. He is thirteen when the novel begins. He is the closest person to Lindsey. Like Lindsey, he is considered exceptionally smart, or "gifted."

Hal Heckler

Samuel's older brother. He dropped out of high school and now owns a motorcycle repair shop. Several of the female characters find him attractive. Samuel and

Buckley look up to him. Hal becomes close to the Salmons because of his brother's relationship with Lindsey.

Mr. Botte

Susie's biology teacher; also her favorite teacher. His daughter is sick with Leukemia and dies not long after Susie is killed.

Mrs. Stead

A woman from the Salmon's neighborhood, and a therapist. While at the crime scene, she identifies Susie's copy of *To Kill a Mockingbird*.

Mrs. Delminico

The home economics teacher at the junior high.

Franny

Susie's intake counselor in heaven. When she was living she worked as a social worker.

Artie

A kid at school who would pretend to inject people with embalming fluid. Later he is at the Gifted Symposium with Lindsey and Samuel and is somewhat of a loner.

Clarissa

Susie's best friend in life.

Nate

Buckley's close friend as a child.

Mrs. Dewitt

The English teacher at the junior high.

Clive Saunders

A boy in Susie's grade who is said to walk like a girl

Phoebe Hart

A girl in Susie's grade who is taunted because of her large breasts.

Mr. Dewitt

The boys' soccer coach. Lindsey is fond of him because he encouraged her to try out for the team and lets her play on the team with the guys.

Principal Caden

Principal of the junior high

The O'Dwyers

The Salmons' neighbors. They have a gazebo that Susie likes. Also, Mr. O'Dwyer can sometimes be heard singing Irish ballads.

Bethel Utemeyer

Formerly a senile neighbor of the Salmons. Now she is the oldest member of Susie's heaven.

Holly

Susie's best friend in heaven. She chose her name from the movie *Breakfast at Tiffany's*.

The Gilberts

The Salmons' neighbors. Their dog finds Susie's elbow.

The Tarkings

The Salmons' neighbors. They have a daughter, Grace, who goes to private school.

The Flanagans

The family who lives in the house by the sinkhole.

Joe Ellis

A boy from the Salmons' neighborhood. He is said to hurt animals and kill animals, but the true culprit was Mr. Harvey. Joe is sent to the military when he is a teenager.

Cleo

The janitor at the junior high.

Mr. Morton

Ray's homeroom teacher, known to have a perpetual hangover

Mr. Peterford

The discipline officer at the junior high

Miss Ryan

The art teacher that transferred to their school from a Catholic school and is more conservative than the last art teachers.

Mrs. Kaplan

The social sciences teacher.

Dr. Singh

Ray's father and a professor.

Reverend Strick

The pastor at the Salmons' church.

Miss Koekle

Buckley's kindergarten teacher.

Claire

A girl who almost became one of Mr. Harvey's victims. She was not killed—he let her go but kept the heel of her shoe.

Sophie Cichetti

One of Mr. Harvey's victims. She was forty-nine years old and she was Mr. Harvey's landlady. After they made love he smashed her skull in and left her body by a creek in Pennsylvania in 1960.

Jackie Meyer

One of Mr. Harvey's victims. She was thirteen years old and was killed in Delaware in 1967.

Flora Hernandez

One of Mr. Harvey's victims. She was eight years old and was killed in Delaware in 1963.

Leah Fox

One of Mr. Harvey's victims. She was twelve years old, and was killed in Delaware in 1969. He fell asleep on top of her after he raped her and she suffocated.

Leidia Johnson

One of Mr. Harvey's victims. She was six years old, was the youngest of his victims, and was killed in Buck's County Pennsylvania. He lured her into a cave he built inside a hill.

Wendy Richter

One of Mr. Harvey's victims. She was thirteen years old and was killed in Connecticut in 1971. She was raped and strangled.

Ralph Cichetti

Sophie Cichetti's son. He tells Hal Heckler he thinks his mother was killed by a boarder who made dollhouses; Hal connects this to Susie's murderer.

Nurse Eliot

The nurse at the hospital that helped Jack both times he was there—after the baseball bat incident and the heart attack.

Major Themes

Loss / Physical and Psychological Absence

When Susie is killed her body is almost completely disposed of, save one elbow. Her family feels the physical loss of her body and the uncertainty of her death, making it difficult for them to mourn her loss. Her family members try to hold on to Susie's belongings to keep her physically with them, but in the end they realize that Susie lives in their memories rather than in objects. In the wake of Susie's death, her mother grows farther away from the family and is psychologically distant from her children and husband. She eventually chooses to also physically remove herself from the home. She is the absent mother and the absent wife, and both Buckley and Jack feel this force tremendously. While Buckley steels himself against missing his mother, Jack falls in love with Abigail again while she is away.

Other characters that experience loss: George Harvey's mother leaves his family when he is very young, and this has a lasting effect on him. Len Fenerman feels the absence of his wife, who committed suicide soon after they were married. Ruana Singh feels the physical and psychological absence of her husband, who has absorbed himself so deeply in his work that he is no longer available to her as a husband. As a counter to the absences felt throughout the novel, Ruth feels the presence of the dead all around her and seeks places where women and girls have been murdered—she feels a spiritual presence in their absence.

Isolation

Many of the characters in the novel are isolated from the rest of society. Susie is trapped in the "perfect world" of her heaven and is thus isolated from her living family and friends. Because she has the desire to watch her loved ones as they change and grow, she also is not able to be with her dead grandfather, who has moved on from watching the living. Susie tries to escape her isolation from Earth by continuously pushing on what she calls the "Inbetween" so she can still influence the world of the living. Susie's immediate family members all isolate themselves in their grieving instead of discussing the loss of Susie openly; for example, each surviving family member goes into Susie's old room alone to grieve her absence. Abigail in particular is portrayed as being alone because she has buried the true Abigail beneath the façade of motherhood. George Harvey is so peculiar that he purposely isolates himself from society, and people find him so strange that they do not usually take the time to associate with him; this allows him to lead a reclusive and secretive lifestyle. Ruth is also isolated, and is described as "haunted" because of her experience with Susie's soul as she left the earth. For many of the characters, this isolation does not allow them room to grow or to recover from their grief. Ruth at first is haunted not by choice, but later chooses to continue her haunted lifestyle when she moves to New York. There she spends her free time seeking out places in the city where violence was committed against girls and women and she takes solace in her isolation. Mr. Harvey is unable to grow out of his isolation as well, but unlike Ruth, he is in a more stagnant place: he is stuck in a traumatic period in his childhood and does not take responsibility for the crimes he committed.

Guilt and Responsibility

When Susie goes missing, her parents feel tremendous guilt. Susie's father bears the brunt of this guilt, because he feels he was not able to be there for his daughter when she needed him. Thus he feels responsible for finding her killer and avenging her death. Len Fenerman also feels guilt over the unsolved cases, including Susie's case and his wife's suicide. Len's guilt escalates when he realizes he let Susie's killer escape because was preoccupied with Abigail. Susie's mother feels a different sort of guilt—she feels guilty for not wanting to be a mother and for wanting to forget about the murder rather than face it. Because Lindsey's parents are locked into their own private grief and guilt, Lindsey feels she must take on the responsibility of parenting. She plays the roll of parent to both Buckley and to her father, who she treats as fragile. Ruth also feels the responsibility of ownership over Susie's story, and to know about her life and her death.

This responsibility then extends to other victims of violence; Ruth feels she has the responsibility to acknowledge the places in New York where violence has been committed. In heaven, Susie also feels the responsibility to take care of her family by pushing past the Inbetween and giving them signs that she is watching them. When Susie sleeps with Ray via Ruth's body, Susie passes on an awareness of the dead to Ray; she instills in him the belief that the dead are all around him and that not everything can be explained by science.

The Power of Photographs

Photographs pause time and capture one moment, and the truth of the image captured is not questioned. Throughout the novel, photographic images are a focus—particularly the pictures that Susie took of Abigail, and Susie's school picture taken before her death. Susie's photos of Abigail serve to liberate her from her roles as mother and wife. In the photograph that Susie takes of Abigail as she looks out over the lawn, before the family is awake, Susie sees her mother as the true Abigail, who she thinks of as the mother-stranger. The camera has the ability to capture the moment when Abigail is her true self.

For each person who sees the picture of Abigail, they have a different reaction. After Susie's death, Jack Salmon develops some of the other rolls of film and finds photographs of Abigail "putting on her mask" as he comes home from work. The mask of motherhood and marriage disguises the real Abigail, and is most visible in the photographs Susie took of her. These photographs also have the power to elicit strong emotional responses from the character that views the photograph. There are other pictures that play some role in the story as well. However, there are no full family pictures, indicating a lack of cohesion in the Salmon family.

The other picture that plays an important role is Susie's school portrait. Len Fenerman keeps a copy of the photo in his wallet as an unsolved case; Abigail keeps a copy in her wallet that she rarely looks at; and Ray keeps a copy that he buries in a volume of Indian poetry, only to discover it again when he goes to college. For Len, the photo represents his failure to deliver justice, and in the end he writes "gone" on the back indicating his acceptance that the dead are no longer with them. For Abigail, Susie is her first daughter and the one who originally made her a mother; the picture makes her feel as though she was punished for not wanting Susie. In the end Abigail leaves the portrait at the airport, symbolizing her transition out of the trauma of Susie's death. For Ray, Susie's picture is an image of the girl that he first loved, and the first lips that he kissed. The photograph represents Susie's absence from Ray and Abigail's lives, and the absence of her body. As the novel goes on, the characters that possess the portrait change their reading of it, symbolizing their ability to move on from the trauma of Susie's death.

Memory

Memory is vital to Susie and to the people she watches. They are important for Susie because her memories are all she has left of her own time on earth. The memories of others are also significant to Susie because in heaven she can see what the people on earth are thinking. For example, watching George Harvey's memories of his mother gives her insight into his disrupted childhood and into the reasons he is a killer. She can also see that he makes an effort not to kill children by killing smaller animals. Susie knows she lives in the memories of the people who knew her. In heaven, she watches for the moments when people think of her and when they speak of her. After a while she realizes that she belongs in their memories and does not always need to be spoken about.

Construction and Destruction

There are a number of places that are constructed in the novel. The first is the underground room that George Harvey builds to kill Susie. In addition, Mr. Harvey makes dollhouses for a living. He also constructs a tent with Jack Salmon. Although Mr. Harvey enjoys construction, he also enjoys the act of destruction: he kills and destroys the bodies of small animals and of girls and women. The sinkhole where Mr. Harvey deposits Susie's body is a physical manifestation of this theme; it is the "mouth" and "throat" of the earth and can swallow and destroy items. Even when developers fill the sinkhole, it is later said to swallow cars whole. The construction of surrounding neighborhoods and industrial lots are in the background of the story, and allow the author to represent the changing environment of the characters as they cope with Susie's death and build anew. Both destructing and constructing are representative of surviving grief and loss for all of the characters. In the end, Lindsey and Samuel find an old house and restore it, literally and figuratively building a new life after Susie is gone.

Surviving Grief

Each character has a different way of recovering from Susie's death. Susie watches her family as they live through the painful experience of losing a daughter/sister, and how it affects each person. Jack wants to avenge Susie's death by finding her killer. Jack also finds himself so absorbed in loving Susie that he has to remind himself to give his love to the living. Lindsey wants to live away from the shadow of Susie. Buckley wants to be let in on the secret of Susie's death, and when he is, he allows himself to miss her and to honor her. Abigail does not want to face Susie's death and instead pulls away from her family and retreats into herself. Susie's family is torn apart in their own separate grieving, but they are able to come back together in the end as a whole, albeit somewhat damaged and in need of healing. Susie also watches Ruth and Ray as they learn how to cope with Susie's loss and form a friendship.

In the end of the novel, Susie notes the formation of new connections, which she refers to as the lovely bones that grew in her absence. These connections allowed her family and friends to survive the grief of losing her. Interestingly, Susie is also able to "survive" her grief at being taken out of the human world and missing her family. By leaving her family in the end, Susie leaves them to live their lives and to move on from her death.

Glossary of Terms

Anecdote

A short account of an interesting incident or event, often biographical.

Aperitif

An alcoholic drink taken before a meal to stimulate the appetite.

Assiduous

Showing great care and perseverance.

Audacity

Boldness or daring, especially with confident or arrogant disregard for personal safety, conventional thought, or other restrictions.

Benzedrine

An amphetamine, or stimulant. One of the frequent side effects of taking such drugs is weight loss.

Borne

Past tense of bear: to carry or transport.

Cease

Come to an end.

Circumscribed

Restricted by limits.

Demean

Something or someone that causes a loss of dignity.

Evensong

Traditionally, Evensong is a Christian service of evening prayers, psalms and canticles. For Susie, Evensong is the time when she surrounds herself with dogs and with music played by the other occupants of her heaven.

Foolhardy

Recklessly bold or rash.

Hyperaware

Informed and alert.

Inextricable

Impossible to disentangle or separate.

Malevolent

Having or showing a wish to do evil to others.

Marvel

To be filled with wonder or astonishment.

Obsequious

Excessively obedient or attendant.

Ostracize

To exclude someone from society or a group.

Perpetual

Continuing forever.

Petulant

Childishly sulky or bad-tempered.

Punt

A delay in answering or taking action.

Spunk

Courage or spirit.

Subjugation

To make submissive.

Tenuous

Very weak or slight.

The Inbetween

The place that Susie defines as being between heaven and Earth. When Susie occupies that space she is sometimes able to communicate with people on Earth.

Transfiguration

in reference to the Transfiguration of Jesus Christ, where Christ appears in radiant glory to three of his disciples. It can also mean a complete change of form or appearance into a more beautiful or spiritual state.

Ubiquitous

Present, appearing, or found everywhere.

Vengeance

Infliction of injury, harm, humiliation, or the like, on a person by someone who has been harmed by that person; violent revenge.

Wedgwood

Ceramic ware made by a man with that name in the 1700s. Most famous for powder blue stoneware with white embossed cameos.

Wrought

Bring about; produce as a result.

Short Summary

Susie Salmon is killed on December 6, 1973 by her family's neighbor, George Harvey. Mr. Harvey lures Susie into a hole he dug in the cornfield. When she tries to leave he rips off her clothes, gags her with her hat and rapes her. He kills her, cuts her up, and puts her in a bag that he takes with him before he fills in the hole. He puts the bag with her body in a safe and takes the safe to the local sinkhole.

When Susie gets to heaven she observes her family. Susie soon realizes that everyone has different heavens that fit what each person wants. She is grateful that Len Fenerman, the detective assigned to her case, is helping them. Upon finding Susie's elbow, the police search the cornfield and find the hole and some of Susie's belongings. Len Fenerman delivers the news to the Salmons that there is too much blood in the earth and they believe Susie is dead. In heaven, Susie watches her family from her gazebo. She looks at a picture that her little brother Buckley drew. In the picture there is a thick blue line separating the earth and the sky; Susie thinks of this space as the Inbetween, and believes it really exists.

When Susie's soul was leaving the earth, she accidentally touched a girl named Ruth Connors. Because of this experience, Ruth becomes fascinated with Susie's life and her death. Susie watches a number of people on earth, including Ruth, Susie's family and her crush Ray Singh. Susie recalls a picture she took of her mother, Abigail, where she is alone and staring out into the yard and has not yet taken on her daily role as mother and wife. Lindsey finds the photograph in Susie's room. Susie's father, Jack, smashes all of the model ships he made. Susie used to help him make the ships, and she breaks the Inbetween by casting her face into the shards of glass.

Not long after Susie's death, Mr. Harvey decides to build a tent outside of his house. Jack Salmon sees him and offers to help. Jack gets the feeling that Mr. Harvey knows something about Susie's murder, and suspects him. He tells Len Fenerman, who goes to Mr. Harvey's house to interview him but does not find him suspicious.

On Christmas, a boy named Samuel Heckler comes to visit Lindsey. He gives her a necklace and they kiss. Susie remembers one day she was late to school and she sat with Ray in the scaffolding in the theater, but the entrance of Ruth Connors interrupted them and they did not kiss. Later that week, Ray kissed Susie by her locker. After Susie's death, Ruth regularly walks the cornfield before school. Ray notices and joins her; they become friends. Jack Salmon goes to the Singhs' to talk to Ray. There he meets Ray's mother Ruana Singh, and he confides in her that he knows who killed Susie.

Grandma Lynn comes to town for Susie's memorial. She brings some light back to the Salmon household. At the memorial Lynn points out George Harvey to Lindsey and she faints. That summer, Lindsey, Samuel and Ruth go to a camp for gifted students. There, Lindsey and Samuel lose their virginity together. The final competition at camp is how to complete the perfect murder.

Susie watches Mr. Harvey and can see into his childhood, when his mother left the family.

His house is exactly like hers, but more barren. He spends a lot of time making dollhouses. Jack Salmon hopes to find clues about Mr. Harvey and constantly calls the police station to report trivial facts about the man. Finally, Len Fenerman comes to their house and tells them they are no longer pursuing the investigation of Susie's murder. That night Jack sees a light in the cornfield; he thinks it is Mr. Harvey so he goes out with a baseball bat. It turns out to be Susie's friend and her boyfriend, and Jack gets beaten up and goes to the hospital. There, Abigail begins an affair with Len Fenerman. Susie knows that Abigail never wanted to be a mother, and she is trying to find a way to escape from Susie's death by having this affair.

When Jack gets home his leg is still stiff. Abigail becomes absorbed in her role as mother yet she distances herself from her children. Lynn comes to visit on Thanksgiving and notices something is different with Abigail, but realizes she can only support her in whatever she decides to do.

Lindsey starts to share her father's suspicion of George Harvey so she breaks into his house and finds a drawing of the hole where he killed Susie. Mr. Harvey comes home and Lindsey narrowly escapes out the window. Mr. Harvey calls the police to report a break-in. Meanwhile, Abigail has met up with Len Fenerman at the mall and they consummate their affair. That night George Harvey leaves town, and later Len realizes he missed his chance to catch him.

The one-year anniversary of Susie's death arrives, and some of her classmates hold a service for her in the cornfield. Abigail does not want to go, but Jack, Buckley and Lindsey go. The following summer Abigail leaves the family and ends up working at a winery in California. Grandma Lynn comes to stay with Jack to help him with the kids and the house. Buckley gets older, and decides to build a fort in the back yard to commemorate Susie. Len Fenerman now believes that George Harvey committed the murder but he cannot find him; in other states, clues begin to link him to other murders.

Lindsey and Samuel graduate from college and decide they want to get married and move into an old house they found. Not long afterwards, Jack has a heart attack and has to go to the hospital. Abigail comes back for the first time in over five years. She realizes she is still in love with Jack and slowly decides she will stay.

Ruth Connors comes back to her hometown because she wants to see the sinkhole before developers close it up. She asks Ray to go with her. When they are there, Susie is watching and manages to break the Inbetween and live in Ruth's body for a few hours. During this time, she makes love to Ray Singh.

The next day, Jack Salmon goes home with his family. Ray and Ruana Singh come over for a visit. While watching them Susie realizes she is grateful for the relationships that grew up in her absence—she refers to these as the lovely bones. Susie decides she is done watching the living, and knows they can move on.

After Susie leaves them, Abigail and Jack stay together in the house and openly talk about Susie when they think of her. Susie goes to a new place in heaven where she has things she never dreamed of in her first, smaller, heaven. There, Susie watches Mr. Harvey die by falling into a ravine. He was never caught. Lindsey and Samuel get married and have a daughter they name Abigail Suzanne. Susie knows she never really grew up but feels she almost has.

Quotes and Analysis

There was only one picture in which my mother was Abigail. It was the first one, the one taken of her unawares, the one captured before the click startled her into mother of the birthday girl, owner of the happy dog, wife to the loving man, and mother again to another girl and a cherished boy. Homemaker. Gardener. Sunny neighbor. My mother's eyes were oceans, and inside them there was loss.

Susie, p. 43

Susie's mother is only her true self when she thinks no one is looking. The loss that Susie sees in her eyes is Abigail's grief over losing herself to the numerous roles listed; she has so many roles to fill in her family life that she does not have time for the real Abigail. Susie uses a metaphor to compare her mother's eyes to "oceans"; like the ocean, her eyes seem deep and endless, and there is no knowing what is inside of them. Susie is not the only one who sees the oceans in her mother's eyes; Jack and Len also see them, and that is part of the reason they both find her so appealing. Susie also finds the mysterious part of her mother appealing, hence the reason she took the picture, but she also does not completely understand it. As the novel goes on, the picture is seen by many characters; their interpretations, along with Susie's new point-of-view in heaven, help Susie to understand the mystery of her mother.

Every day he got up. Before sleep wore off, he was who he used to be. Then, as his consciousness woke, it was as if poison seeped in. At first he couldn't even get up. He lay there under a heavy weight, But then only movement could save him, and he moved and he moved and he moved, no movement being enough to make up for it. The guilt on him, the hand of God pressing down on him saying, You were not there when your daughter needed you.

Susie, p. 59

Each morning Jack feels as though poison seeps in when he remembers what happened to his daughter. The poison is a metaphor for the grief and guilt Jack feels over Susie's death. The poison also references an earlier use of the word, when Susie described how rabbits sometimes accidentally eat poison and then bring it back to their dens, poisoning the entire rabbit family. Similarly, the grief and guilt that result from Susie's death is a sort of "poison" for all of the Salmons, as it has infected their entire family. When Jack wakes up in the morning he has a feeling that he is under a heavy weight; this feeling parallels Susie's experience with Mr. Harvey—after he raped her she lies under his weight and realizes she is still alive. Jack also realizes that he is still alive, and it is movement that saves him, because movement is something only the living can do. Susie, on the other hand, was unable to move even after Mr. Harvey gets up. The hand of God pressing down on Jack indicates that Jack feels pressure to avenge Susie's death to make up for the fact that he was not able to be there to prevent it.

Len Fenerman had been the first one who had asked my mother for my school picture when the police thought I might be found alive. In his wallet, my photo sat in a stack. Among these dead children and strangers was a picture of his wife. If a case had been solved he had written the date of its resolution on the back of the photo. If the case was still open—in his mind, not in the official files of the police—it was blank. There was nothing on the back of mine. There was nothing on the back of his wife's.

Susie, p. 90

Len is particularly affected by the loss of his wife when they had just gotten married. Her picture in his wallet is significant because it is among the pictures of the cases that he solves as a professional, yet his wife's case is personal. Thus, Len is not able to keep his personal and professional life separate, which is apparent in his later intimate interaction with Abigail. When he is not able to solve a case such as Susie's, he feels personally responsible. For Len, a case is still open if it has not been solved, even if the police have closed the case. Also, the case of his wife is not a police case, as we later find out that she committed suicide, and thus Len will probably never be able to "solve" her case. His job is to survive the grief of losing her. Absence is represented by the blank in the back of the photos. However, solving the cases does not negate the fact that the people in the photographs are no longer living. The physical loss of them is recorded later when Len writes "gone" on the backs of all of the photos.

What did dead mean, Ray wondered. It meant lost, it meant frozen, it meant gone. He knew that no one ever really looked the way they did in photos. He knew he didn't look as wild or as frightened as he did in his own. He came to realize something as he stared at my photo—that it was not me.

Susie, p. 112

Ray Singh uses Susie's photograph as a way of saying goodbye to her. Ray muses on the meaning of death, expanding on the theme of loss—Susie's body is lost to her family, she will always be frozen in time at age fourteen, and she is gone from the world of the living. His realization that the photograph is not Susie is similar to a realization that Susie had as a child. When Susie went to see Mrs. Utemeyer's body at the funeral, she saw that the corpse was Mrs. Utemeyer but it also was not. For Ray, the picture is the closest thing to a corpse; Susie does not exist in the picture, and she does not exist on Earth either. She is, as he put it, gone. Directly after this Ray figuratively buries the photograph. Thus his use of the photograph as a grave for Susie parallels Len's and Abigail's use of it (the two other characters who keep the same photograph with them).

"When the dead are done with the living," Franny said to me, "the living can go on to other things."

"What about the dead?" I asked. "Where do we go?"

She wouldn't answer me.

Susie and Franny, p. 145

This quote exemplifies the theme of surviving grief. Susie must accept that she is dead and that she is no longer part of the human world; she too is grieving the loss of her life. Susie's grief parallels the grief of her family as they try to continue with their lives after her murder. Franny's advice foreshadows Susie's future in heaven, when she will no longer watch the living. However, Susie is not yet ready to do this, and the idea of leaving her family scares her because she does not know where she will go if she leaves them. She is still maturing towards a point where she can accept her death and let her family build a new life without her.

Each time I told my story, I lost a bit, the smallest drop of pain. It was that day that I knew I wanted to tell the story of my family. Because horror on earth is real and it is every day. It is like the flower or like the sun; it cannot be contained.

Susie, p. 186

Throughout the novel, many of the characters feel trapped: Susie is trapped in heaven, Ruth feels trapped in a hell on earth, Abigail feels trapped in her life as a mother. But here, Susie exposes the fact that horror cannot be contained; she uses a simile to compare horror to a flower and to the sun. When the sun is out, there is no capturing or containing it. Within each of the places that the characters feel trapped, horror still infiltrates, much like the sun can filter through nooks and crannies. By meeting the other girls who were also Mr. Harvey's victims, she can relieve some of her pain by telling the story of her family. The novel is the story of her family, and thus it is part of Susie's way of "surviving" her grief and alleviating her pain.

Lindsey and Buckley had come to live their lives in direct proportion to what effect it would have on a fragile father.

Susie, p. 244

Both Lindsey and Buckley feel the responsibility to protect their father; this responsibility parallels the feeling that Jack has that he is responsible for avenging Susie's death. Here Jack is described as fragile because he is both physically and emotionally fragile. He is emotionally broken from Susie's death and from Abigail's absence. He is still physically handicapped from the knee replacement surgery, and he also now has slower reaction times. These factors combine to make him very sensitive to stress, hence the reason that Lindsey and Buckley feel the need to protect him. In some ways, they have become the parents, and Jack the child.

After eight years it was, even for my mother, like the ubiquitous photo of a celebrity. She had encountered it so many times that I had been neatly buried inside of it. My cheeks never redder, my eyes never bluer than they were in the photograph.

Susie, p. 265

Just as Ray chose to figuratively bury Susie's photograph in a book, Abigail feels that Susie is buried inside the photograph. By keeping her buried there, she does not have to look at her, or miss her. Sebold uses a simile to compare Susie's photograph to that of a celebrity, implying that the photograph is seen so often that Abigail has become almost numbed to it, yet it is also something she is drawn toward. Comparing Susie to a celebrity also connotes the fact that Susie is not someone with whom Abigail has intimate contact. Instead, she must admire her from afar. The hyperbole that Susie's cheeks and eyes are more vibrant in this picture than they ever were in life reminds the reader that photography is not always the most realistic depiction of a person; despite this, the photograph still holds some power for Abigail.

And there she was again, alone and walking out in the cornfield while everyone else I cared for sat together in one room. She would always feel me and think of me. I could see that, but there was no longer anything I could do. Ruth had been a girl haunted and now she would be a woman haunted. First by accident and now by choice. All of it, the story of my life and death, was hers if she chose to tell it, even to one person at a time.

Susie, p. 321

Ruth is an outsider throughout the novel, and she continues to be one until the end. Although she does form a connection with Ray, she feels more connected to the dead than to the living. In high school Ruth did not choose to isolate - she was simply an outsider because of her habits - but as she grows up she chooses to isolate. Although Ruth's character matures along with the rest of the characters, she still maintains a "haunted" quality. Susie now accepts that she cannot help Ruth, but that Ruth now has the ability to help her by telling Susie's story on earth.

These were the lovely bones that had grown around my absence: the connections—sometimes tenuous, sometimes made at great cost, but often magnificent—that happened after I was gone. And I began to see things in a way that let me hold the earth without me in it. The events that my death wrought were merely the bones of a body that would become whole at some unpredictable time in the future. The price of what I came to see as this miraculous body had been my life.

Susie, p. 320

The lovely bones of the title are explained here; although we may have expected the title to be referring to Susie's bones, it actually refers to the "bones" that have metaphorically grown up in Susie's absence. Susie may not have a body on earth, but the connections made between the people she loves constitute a symbolic body. Without her death, these relationships would not exist. Seeing these lovely bones help Susie to recover from her own death and move on, leaving the human world. She is grateful for the "body" and she knows it could not have existed without her. This body has also helped her loved ones recover from the grief of losing her; it is a support system for them as they grow stronger in the wake of her death leave Susie to their memories.

Summary and Analysis of Epigraph & Chapters 1-3

Epigraph

Susie describes a snow globe that sat on her father's desk when she was a child. The snow globe contained a penguin. Susie worried the penguin was alone; her father reassured her by saying that the penguin has a nice life because he is trapped in a perfect world.

Chapter 1

The narrator, Susie Salmon, opens the chapter by giving her name and the date of her murder—December 6, 1973. She compares herself to the other missing girls of the seventies—all of them are white with mousy brown hair.

Susie introduces her killer as a man in the neighborhood. She knew of him because her mother liked his border flowers, and her father once had a conversation with him about fertilizer. The day that Susie is killed, she is walking home from school through the cornfield in the snow. It is after dark. George Harvey startles her. He tells her he built something and asks if she wants to come see it. She tries to excuse herself to go home, but he insists and calls her by her name even though she hasn't told him her name. At the time she thought maybe he knew it because her father frequently talks about how Susie tried to pee on Lindsey when Lindsey was a baby because Susie was so jealous. However, Susie's father never told Mr. Harvey this story. Later Mr. Harvey even asks Susie's mother what her name was while offering his condolences. Susie is outraged by Mr. Harvey's actions. Susie's intake counselor in heaven, Franny, is not.

Susie follows Mr. Harvey to the place he built. She notices he looks at her strangely, like other men have since she matured; but she also notes that men do not usually look at her like this when she is in her yellow elephant bellbottoms and her royal blue parka. Mr. Harvey has made a dugout beneath the earth, and he leads Susie down into it. Susie is really impressed by the hideout. It is a small room, with benches and shelves. The shelves have a mirror, shaving cream and a razor. Susie thinks this is odd, but she passes it off as part of Mr. Harvey being what her dad would call "a character."

Susie jumps ahead a little, to after her death, after Mr. Harvey has closed up the hole. Susie is not able to observe her family until three days later, when she looks in at her mother, who is very pale. Her father, on the other hand, wants to help the cops find Susie's killer. Susie is grateful for Len Fenerman, the detective on her case, because he is able to help keep her father busy.

Inside the hole, Mr. Harvey pressures Susie into having a Coke. He tells her he built the dugout as a clubhouse for neighborhood kids, but she knows he is lying. He tells her she is pretty, and Susie describes how he gives her the "skeevies." She tries to leave but he blocks the exit and demands that she take off all of her clothes so he can check to see if she is still a virgin. She fights him but he overpowers her and undresses her. Susie thinks about her mother and how she will be wondering where she is. Mr. Harvey begins to kiss Susie. Susie thinks of her only other kiss, with the boy she likes, Ray Singh. Susie begs Mr. Harvey by saying, "Don't" and "please." He puts her hat in her mouth. Susie cries. Mr. Harvey rips open her pants and rapes her. Susie can hear her mother calling her to dinner while Mr. Harvey is inside her. When he is done Susie is surprised she is still alive, but she knows he will kill her. He tells her to get up. She cannot. Mr. Harvey gets a knife. He asks Susie to tell her she loves him. She does but he kills her anyway.

Chapter 2

When Susie first gets to heaven she thinks everyone's heaven is like hers. Her heaven has soccer goal posts and the buildings are suburban high schools, like Fairfax High where Susie would have gone the next year. Susie imagines that she would be beautiful and popular in high school, and that she would protect other kids from being teased. After Susie has been in heaven awhile she realizes that the other people in her heaven are people whose heavens have some of the same elements as hers does. Susie meets an Asian girl named Holly and they become friends. Susie describes heaven as a place where they are given their simplest dreams; whatever they desired, they got. What Holly and Susie really want is to grow up, but they are not able to experience that.

Susie's father gets a phone call on the evening of December 9th from Detective Fenerman, who reports they found one of Susie's body parts. Susie's mother makes a list of all the things Susie carried with her in hopes that it will help in the investigation. Susie's parents do not know how to comfort each other. Susie watches them as they try to console one another. She then looks at the cornfields where she knows there are rabbits living in warrens; sometimes, a rabbit will unknowingly bring home poison and all of the family will die in their den.

In the morning Lindsey asks what the phone call was about. Her father tells her they found a body part. Lindsey wants to know which body part even though she knows it will make her sick. Her father gets her a bowl to throw up in, and he tells her the Gilberts' dog found Susie's elbow; Lindsey promptly vomits.

In the cornfield the police begin a search for Susie's body. They find the place where the dugout was, and dig there. They are disappointed they don't find a body, but later they find out the earth has a lot of Susie's blood in it. Neighbors watch from behind the police lines. The police find a copy of To Kill a Mockingbird, and Mrs. Stead, the only neighbor left watching, identifies it as a book that is read in the ninth grade (Susie's grade). The police inform Susie's parents, but they refuse to believe it. Two days later, the police find Susie's notes from Mr. Botte's class and a love note written to Susie by Ray Singh. Susie never read the note because he had stuck it in her notebook the day she was killed. Ray becomes a suspect. The police soon realize he has an alibi, because he was speaking at a conference for his father that day. Susie is frustrated that she cannot lead the police to her killer. She also misses the family dog Holiday, but does not miss her family in the same way because she cannot accept that she will never see them again.

Len Fenerman comes to visit the Salmons. He delivers the hat that Susie had in her pocket; a hat handmade my Susie's mother, with little bells and pompoms, that Susie refused to wear. Len Fenerman tells the family that the hat was used as a gag. He also says that there is too much blood in the earth, and they now have to work with the assumption that Susie is dead. Len Fenerman leaves, and each family member is in his/her own private grief; Susie's mother sitting on the carpet over the hat, Lindsey standing stiff, and Susie's father going upstairs and sobbing into Holiday's fur. Buckley is with his friend Nate—when Nate's mother comes to return him, she senses something is different and waits a while before bringing him back. Susie's parents decide to call Grandma Lynn (Susie's maternal grandmother) to tell her the sad news.

Lindsey decides to return to school in the one week left before Christmas. Mrs. Dewitt approaches Lindsey and asks her to go to the Principal's office. There, Principal Caden gives her his condolences, but Lindsey resists, asking him what exactly she lost. Susie's recalls when Lindsey tested and labeled gifted, and how she felt she needed to live up to that label. Mr. Caden tells Lindsey that Mr. Dewitt is thinking of coaching a girls' soccer team; Lindsey comments on how the soccer field is very near to where her sister was murdered. That night Lindsey goes home and does sit-ups, push-ups and bicep curls in her room, focusing on her breathing.

In heaven, Susie sits in her gazebo. She thinks about the picture that Buckley drew that was hung on the refrigerator hours before her death. In it, there is a thick blue line separating the air and the ground. Susie calls it the Inbetween, and she wants it to really exist. Because her heaven is filled with things she desires, there are a lot of dogs running around and she and Holly play with them. Mrs. Bethel Utemeyer, the oldest member of Susie's heaven, plays a duet on her violin with Holly on horn. Susie calls this her Evensong.

Chapter 3

Susie describes watching the earth from above, and seeing the souls as they travel. They stop and touch a living person before they leave the earth. When Susie left the earth, she was escaping violence and her path was not calculated. She touched a girl named Ruth Connors who was standing in the school parking lot at the time. Ruth tells her mother about the encounter, calling it a dream that was too real. Her mother just thinks her imagination has run wild. But when Ruth finds out about Susie's death, she starts to investigate. She looks at pictures of Susie in the yearbook. She watches Susie's friend Clarissa, and her boyfriend Brian Nelson. Then Ruth steals things from Clarissa's locker—pictures of Susie and Brian's stash of weed. Ruth gets high and mulls over the pictures.

Susie spends whole days watching people on earth. She watches the teachers at her school and what they do in their personal time, and she watches Clarissa, and Ruth. One day Franny finds Susie shivering—Susie is thinking of her mother. Susie remembers when she turned eleven, and she had just gotten a camera. She woke up early and was taking pictures of a neighborhood girl. Grace Tarking, and pretending to be a wildlife photographer. Then Susie noticed her mother; she snapped a photo of her sitting on the porch and staring into space when she thought no one was watching her. When Susie gets the pictures developed she realizes that that picture is the only one where her mother is really Abigail. She can see why Susie's father calls Abigail "Ocean Eyes." While Susie is thinking about this, Lindsey gets up in the middle of the night and goes to Susie's room. Susie's room remains untouched, the bed still unmade. Lindsey finds the picture of their mother. Susie had never shown it to anyone else because she wanted to be the only one who knew about the "mother-stranger", so Lindsey is surprised by the photo.

Susie used to help her father build model ships. He called her his first mate. Neither Lindsey nor Buckley were as interested in helping him build ships. On December 23, 1973, Susie's father is looking at his ships and remembering Susie. He lines all of the ships up and then smashes them all. This crushes Susie, and without meaning to, she casts her face into every shard of glass. Susie's father laughs deeply. Then he goes to Susie's room with the intention of smashing her mirror and ripping her wallpaper, but instead he falls against the bed and cries into her sheets. Buckley finds him there. Susie's father calls Buckley to him and holds him. Susie's father remembers how Susie used to fall out of bed at night; he also remembers how once, a few weeks before she died, he found Buckley curled up with Susie in bed. Her father sees Susie in Buckley, and tells himself he should give his love to the living.

Analysis

In the epigraph, the world in the snow globe is a supposedly "perfect world." When Susie is in heaven she also refers to her world there as a perfect world, because she has all she desires. While viewing the snow globe, Susie worried that the penguin would be lonely; this fear comes true for Susie in heaven. Even though she is in a perfect world, she is trapped there without the company of her loved ones. This passage exemplifies the theme of isolation.

In Chapter 1, Susie, the protagonist and narrator, is introduced. We learn right away that Susie is narrating the story after her death as a first person point-of-view. She is an omniscient narrator, meaning she knows everything that goes on in all of the characters lives and in their thoughts. Immediately, the reader is asked to suspend disbelief and believe that there is an afterlife, that Susie is in it, and that she is narrating after her death. Even though Susie's narration is omniscient, she is also narrating from the first person—thus, she is involved in the story and has her own emotions and motivations.

Even though the story is about murder, the novel is not a mystery novel. We are introduced to Susie's killer, George Harvey, in the first chapter. Susie gives the context of the murder by giving the time period and the relative location of the suburbs, and noting that murders like this were not common. The rape and murder set the tone for the novel; all of the subsequent events and relationships are a result of the murder. While she is being raped Susie thinks of her first kiss with Ray Singh, foreshadowing the fact that throughout the novel all sex is overshadowed by Susie's experience with Mr. Harvey. During her rape, Susie describes how she feels using simile—she is like a sea, and she also feels like she is being turned inside out like a cat's cradle. By comparing herself to other things, Susie demonstrates that she feels as though she is not in her body. Susie survives the rape, but knows he is going to kill her. As if in acknowledgment of that fact, the knife that Mr. Harvey uses smiles at her.

Mr. Harvey's affinity for both construction of new spaces and for destruction of life and evidence sets up a theme: construction and destruction are naturally equal and opposites, and they continue to oppose each other throughout the novel. The murder starts off the cycle of destruction, as Mr. Harvey kills Susie and cuts up her body and in turn Susie's family begins to fall apart as they deal with the grief.

In Chapter 2, Susie describes how rabbits sometimes bring home poison and the whole family dies inside the dens; the rabbits serve as an allegory for what is going on in Susie's family. The poison for them is the devastation from the loss of Susie; the grief is affecting them all and destroying them by pulling them apart. In addition, the recovery of some of Susie's things, and of the one elbow, leaves the family in pieces as well—each family member is affected differently by the objects/body parts that are found, thus emphasizing the differences in their grieving. Susie's mother is particularly affected by the hat she made for Susie—this is what breaks her. From that point on, Abigail acts numb to Susie's death and begins to reconsider her role as mother. Lindsey does not talk about her grief with anyone, and when the principal at school tries to console her, Lindsey is cold. Jack feels extremely guilty that he was not there to help Susie, and he also feels the responsibility to help Lindsey and Abigail through their grief, but does not know how.

Chapter 2 also introduces the concept of the Inbetween as depicted by Buckley's drawing; the Inbetween plays an important role in the novel, because it is Susie's only way of coming in contact with her family and friends. Chapter 3 marks the first time that Susie is able to break the Inbetween—by casting her face into the shards of her father's destroyed model ships. In the wake of Susie's death, there is much destruction as the family is not yet ready to move on and build a new life without Susie; here, the ships are a symbol of that destruction. Later in the novel, Jack will again consider building ships with his grandchild, as he survives the grief of Susie's loss.

Chapter 3 introduces the powerful effect that a photograph can have, a theme that runs through the novel. After Ruth Connors is touched by Susie's soul, she gets to know Susie through photographs that she finds in the yearbook and in Clarissa's locker. Even though Ruth was not close with Susie while she was living, she feels closer to her after her death by looking at photographs of her. Chapter 3 also includes a description of the photograph that Susie took of Abigail, a photograph that appears repeatedly throughout the novel. This photograph has the power of unmasking Abigail; when Abigail is not aware of anyone else around her, she is the person she was before she took on the role of wife and mother. Susie later refers to the woman in the picture as a mother-stranger, and the mysterious mother, because Susie does not fully know or understand this side of her mother. Both the pictures that Ruth looks at and the picture of Abigail are open to interpretation by the viewer. While the picture may reveal some new information about the subject, it is up to the viewer to decide what she is learning and seeing from the picture, because a picture can have a different meaning for each viewer.

Summary and Analysis of Chapters 4-7

Chapter 4

When Susie first goes missing, her parents go door to door and make phone calls looking for her. In the meantime, Mr. Harvey puts Susie's body parts in a sack and closes up the hole. He carries her back to the house and leaves her in the garage, where her blood leaves a stain on the floor. Inside, Mr. Harvey washes up and is very calm, thinking about Susie's scream and her death moan. In the bag with Susie are the razors, shaving cream, knife and a book of sonnets. Mr. Harvey keeps the knife and the sonnets. Susie compares her desire to know more about Mr. Harvey, about her death, and about the other girls he killed, to the desire dogs have to go after a smell even when it is a bad smell.

Mr. Harvey takes Susie's remains to a sinkhole. Susie remembers going to the sinkhole with her father and Buckley to put an old refrigerator in it. Her father tells Buckley that the sinkhole is the earth's mouth and that it will swallow the refrigerator. Mr. Harvey puts the bag with Susie's remains in a metal safe so that it will weigh it down. The sinkhole is on the Flanagan's property, so he gives them money to sink the safe. On his way home, Mr. Harvey realizes he has Susie's charm bracelet in his pocket. He stops his car and wanders a construction lot in the dark. He decides to keep the Pennsylvania keystone charm, with Susie's initials, and throws the rest of the charm bracelet in a hole that will become a man-made lake.

Mr. Harvey reads about the tents built by a tribe in Mali and decides to replicate them. Susie's father comes upon Mr. Harvey while he is doing this, and he helps him with the tent. After the basic structure is done, Mr. Harvey goes inside and checks on the knife that he used to kill Susie, which is still in his nightstand.

Outside, Susie's father thinks he hears her. She tries to make the dead geranium near him bloom, but it does not. But her father does begin to suspect that Mr. Harvey knows something about Susie's death. He asks Mr. Harvey about it but Mr. Harvey gives no answers.

Chapter 5

Sometimes Susie wishes her father would avenge her death by going after Mr. Harvey, but she knows he is not like that. Instead he feels guilty that he was not able to be there for her. When Susie's father returns from Mr. Harvey's, he looks for Abigail but he cannot find her. Lindsey comes in the house slamming doors and other things; Jack goes to check on her but she says she wants to be alone. Jack calls Len Fenerman to tell him that he suspects Mr. Harvey. Abigail is in the downstairs bathroom sneaking bites from macaroons. Buckley knocks at the door and screams Momma. Abigail realizes she hates the word. While Jack makes fluffernutter sandwiches for them, Buckley asks where Susie is. Jack distracts him by asking him if he wants to go to the zoo.

Len Fenerman goes to George Harvey's house. He had been there before when the police went door-to-door questioning the neighbors and found nothing remarkable there. While there, Mr. Harvey tells Len that he built the tent for his dead wife Leah and that he does it every year, but this is the first year he did it outside. Mr. Harvey suggests that perhaps the Ellis boy was involved in the murder, because he likes to hurt animals. Len has already checked it out and the boy has an alibi. Len calls Jack to report what Mr. Harvey said. Jack says he thought that Mr. Harvey's wife's name was Sophie, as he heard that from Abigail. Jack writes Sophie and Leah in a book—Susie notes that he is unknowingly listing the dead.

On Christmas Samuel Heckler comes to the Salmons' to visit Lindsey. He is thirteen and he is dressed in black leather with his hair slicked back. He tells her he is also one of the gifted students. Buckley is curious about Samuel's suitcase, which is actually an alto saxophone. Buckley then asks where Susie is. Jack takes Buckley to play monopoly. He says the board is the world and the pieces are the people they know. Susie is the shoe because that is what she used to use. Jack tells him when he rolls the dice, one of the pieces can't play anymore. Buckley asks why. Jack tells him Susie is dead and that he won't see her again. Buckley keeps the monopoly shoe in his dresser until it one day goes missing.

Abigail leaves Samuel and Lindsey alone in the kitchen. Lindsey opens the gift that Samuel got her—it is a half of a heart on a necklace. Samuel has the other half. Lindsey kisses him, and Susie watches and feels very alive.

Chapter 6

Two weeks before Susie died, she was late to school. She had never been late, but she knew about how the janitor left the back door to the stage open for the stoners. Susie goes in that door. She sneaks in slowly, then she hears a voice tell her she is beautiful. It is Ray Singh. He is from India and he moved to her town a year ago from England. Susie thinks he is cool and she knows he has a crush on her. Ray is sitting up on the scaffolding. She asks him what he is doing up there, and he invites her to come up. Ray tells her he is skipping English class because he already knows all of Shakespeare. After the bell for first period rings, Ray leans towards her and they are about to kiss when they hear something. Below them Mr. Peterford and Miss Ryan walk in and begin to scold Ruth Connors for a drawing she had done of a naked woman. The drawing was copied and passed around school. The teachers leave and Ruth cries. Ray tells Susie to go to her. Susie notes that later that week Ray kisses her by her locker.

Susie stands in front of Ruth, holding her jungle bell hat in her hand. Ruth tells her it's a stupid hat and Susie agrees. Susie asks to see the drawing, and Ruth shows her that drawing and many more that she has in her notebooks. Susie comments that they are really good; she no longer thinks of Ruth as weird.

Ruth walks in the cornfield after it is roped off, and often skips class to do so. She has her father drive her to school daily to avoid going on the bus. Before she gets out of the car he gives her a sip of bourbon from his thermos, but she usually does not drink any unless he is watching. Susie watches her on those mornings, and grows to love her and felt that they kept each other company from opposites sides of the Inbetween.

Ray notices that Ruth walks in the cornfield a lot, so one day he makes a point of meeting her there and waits for her in the shot-put circle. Ray offers her tea but she refuses. Ruth offers him lip balm because his lips are chapped, and she tells him he can keep it. He asks her to sit with him while the buses come. This becomes a ritual for them, meeting there on the days that Ray's father, a professor, has to teach. They read poetry and talk about the other oddball kids in the class. Sometimes they talk about Susie; Ruth thinks she is lucky to be out of there, Ray thinks where they are is only temporary hell. He suggests Susie is in heaven.

Jack Salmon goes to Ray Singh's house to talk with him. Ray is not home so Jack sits with Ray's mother, Ruana Singh for a while. Jack tells Ruana he knows who killed Susie. Ruana believes that Jack is doing what he knows is right for him, but she hopes it will not harm her son. Ruana goes out to meet Ray and to tell him of his visitor.

While Jack is at the Singhs', Len Fenerman visits. Abigail is left to entertain him alone. She draws stick figures in crayon on butcher paper. Buckley and his friend Nate are asleep on the couch. Len tells Abigail that she reminds him of his wife, who died soon after they were married. Susie's father comes home and Nate and Buckley greet him with high energy. Len has Susie's picture in his wallet along with the pictures of victims from all of the other cases he has worked on; the cases that have been solved have the date written on the back, and the ones that haven't are blank. Both Susie's picture and Len's wife's picture are blank. Jack tells the boys to go upstairs because he wants to talk with Len.

Chapter 7

Buckley and Nate race upstairs. Buckley tells Nate that he sees Susie. Susie says she tries not to yearn for Buckley because she does not want him to see her because she thinks he is too young. Buckley and Nate sit underneath a framed graverubbing by their parents' bedroom. This is one of many, but it is the only one still up. Lindsey and Susie used to play that they were in the rubbing, which pictures a knight and his dog. Lindsey would be his distressed widow. Buckley takes Nate into Susie's room and they go under her bed to her secret hiding place in a hole in her boxspring. There, she kept things she didn't want anyone else to see. After she died, Holiday came and scratched it open, and the things came out. Buckley shows Nate a small bloody twig that Susie kept wrapped in a handkerchief. The summer before, when Buckley was three, Susie was watching him one day when he was playing with Nate. Buckley swallowed the twig and choked. Susie drove him to the hospital because there were no adults around, and she saved his life. Buckley remembers this, and he also remembers how serious and worried the adults looked then; now his parents' eyes looked flat. In heaven Susie sees a row of crows holding crooked twigs. She wonders if Buckley really sees her.

Analysis

While Chapters 1 – 3 presented the initial scenes of destruction create the somber tone and the setting for the novel, Chapters 4 – 6 begin to show how the characters are reacting in the face of loss and absence, and how they have begun to build anew, both physically and figuratively.

Mr. Harvey puts Susie's body is in a safe before he dumps it in the sinkhole. The safe functions as its name prescribes—to keep Susie safe from being found. With Mr. Harvey's discarding of the body we again encounter the theme of destruction, which goes hand in hand with the emotional collapse of Susie's family. To counter this destruction, at the end of Chapter 4 Jack helps Mr. Harvey build a tent. Jack simultaneously builds his own theory that Mr. Harvey is Susie's killer. While Jack looks for Susie's killer, Susie also is "hunting" for the reasons why Mr. Harvey killed her; she uses a metaphor to compare herself to the dogs at Evensong who hunt for something once they smell it, no matter if it is a bad smell or a good one. Susie also does her best to lead her father to Mr. Harvey by pushing on the Inbetween; she is on a personal hunt but she is also on a mission to help her family find her killer. Jack tells Len of his suspicion but Len does not believe—he passes Mr. Harvey off as a character, paralleling Susie's thoughts about Mr. Harvey before she realized she was in danger.

Susie's father's suspicion about who killed Susie and his desire for revenge stems from his guilt that he was unable to be there for his daughter. In the opening of Chapter 5 the word poison is used as a metaphor for the way the feeling of guilt slowly settles in when Jack wakes up. The poison represents the psychological effects of losing Susie, and alludes to the earlier metaphor of the rabbits that bring home poison and die. Lindsey is feeling a different psychological effect from the loss of Susie; she has what Susie refers to as the "Walking Dead Syndrome" because everyone, including Lindsey, sees Susie when they look at her. The effects of loss start to show in Abigail as she begins to resent hearing the word "mother."

The symbols presented in these chapters help to further our understanding of the effects of loss on all of the family members. The monopoly shoe represents Susie and her inability to be a part of the game of life. Buckley keeps the shoe hidden because he is aware that his family is each keeping their own memories and feelings about Susie hidden. The other symbolic presence is the grave rubbing that is hanging in the upstairs hallway of the Salmons' house. A grave is one way of remembering the dead, yet Susie does not have a grave. The image in the rubbing is a knight with his faithful dog at his heels, and Lindsey and Susie used to pretend that Susie was the knight and Lindsey was his bereaved widow. In their role-playing Lindsey would tell the knight that she had to move on. Thus the grave rubbing represents both absence and loss and the necessity to move on.

In order to survive grief, the characters begin to build new relationships with each other. On Christmas, Lindsey and Samuel start their relationship, something that becomes a lasting form of support for Lindsey as she copes with her sister's loss. Buckley also claims to have formed a new relationship with Susie where he is able to talk to her. Buckley's belief that he can see Susie is later recognized as a desire rather than a truth. The relationship the dead have with the living is not always parallel because they are separated by the Inbetween. Interestingly, Buckley is the one who originally drew the picture depicting the Inbetween, giving a visual image to what Susie imagines as her passageway to be with the living.

In addition, Ruth Connors and Ray Singh begin to form a new relationship as one way of coping with Susie's absence. When Susie was living, there is one scene where Ruth, Ray and Susie are all in the same room together, and Susie is the one who interacts with both of them but Ruth and Ray do not interact with each other. During this scene, they are all represented doing forbidden things (i.e. Ray and Susie are skipping class, and Ruth drew a naked picture), and are cast as outsiders. This outsider status of these characters continues through the novel, because all of them are isolated in their own way. Ruth and Ray meet again in the cornfield after Susie's death—there they form a friendship where they can discuss why and how they feel like outsiders, and seek to understand Susie's death and her potential afterlife.

Summary and Analysis of Chapters 8-11

Chapter 8

Mr. Harvey dreams of buildings. His favorite is Vologda, The Church of Transfiguration. This is what he dreams about before he has the "not still" dreams of women and children. In George Harvey's childhood, his father was a builder—making houses in the desert of glass and wood. When he has the not still dreams, he looks through his father's notebooks. He thinks of his mother the last time he saw her, dressed in white and running through a field after his father forced her out of the car. She had given George her amber necklace on her way out.

Chapter 9

Grandma Lynn comes for Susie's memorial service in a limousine and wearing a mink around her neck. Lynn has Jack make her a drink; when she finds out Jack is not drinking, she gets him to drink with her. Susie realizes that Lynn is bringing the light back to their house. Lynn tells Abigail she needs help, and insists on giving her a make-over with her "bag o' magic." Lindsey asks Grandma Lynn to teach her about make-up. She tells her about it while she does Abigail's make-up. When Lindsey suddenly thinks of Samuel Heckler, Grandma Lynn knows immediately from Lindsey's expression that she has a boyfriend. Lynn does Lindsey's make-up and she looks like a clown. Jack gets drunk, and Abigail goes to bed without doing the dishes, which is not usual for her. After everyone is in bed, Lindsey looks at herself in the mirror. Both Lindsey and Susie see an adult who can take care of herself. Lindsey makes faces at herself in the mirror, and then sleeps on her back so as not to mess up her face.

Mrs. Bethel Utemeyer was the only dead person Lindsey and Susie had ever seen. She moved in with her son in their neighborhood when Lindsey was five and Susie was six. Sometimes she would leave the house and get lost. Abigail would bring her in for tea, and she would be there when Lindsey and Susie got home. She often called Lindsey "Natalie." When she died, Lindsey and Susie were excited to view the body. Their mother was pregnant with Buckley at the time. Mr. Utemeyer took them up to see the body, and told his mother that he brought her Natalie. Both girls thought she might talk. Susie noted that "it" (the body) was Mrs. Utemeyer, but that it was something else as well. Mrs. Utemeyer is in Susie's heaven, and she walks hand in hand with a little blond girl, her daughter Natalie.

The morning of the memorial, Lindsey decides she will wear one of Susie's dresses. She goes into her room and opens the closet. Grandma Lynn comes in and asks Lindsey to help her with zipping and hooking her dress. Lynn tells Lindsey she is pretty, which is a shock to Lindsey since Lynn never gives out compliments. Lynn helps Lindsey pick out a dress, and she picks a mini dress that belonged to Clarissa. While Lynn is looking, Lindsey asks Lynn who the man is that her father thinks did it. She doesn't answer. She is so busy helping Lindsey that she doesn't put make-up on.

Samuel Heckler is at the church waiting for them. Detective Fenerman is there as well. Susie wishes she could be there with her father. He feels every day he wakes up there is something else to get through. Ruth comes to the service as well. She is with her father. She notes Lindsey's new look and doesn't like it because she thinks make-up is demeaning. She also notices Hal Heckler in the graveyard smoking. Clarissa is at the service with Brian Nelson. She approaches the Salmons and offers her condolences. Abigail is angry because Clarissa is alive and Susie is not. Clarissa notices Lindsey is wearing her dress but realizes she will never get it back. Ray Singh does not come; he says good-bye to Susie by looking at the portrait she had given him earlier that year. He realizes the photo is not her and that Susie exists in the things he does rather than in the picture. He places the picture in a volume of Indian poetry where he and his mother press flowers.

At the service people say nice things about Susie. Grandma Lynn points out George Harvey to Lindsey and she looks at him and then faints. Mr. Harvey then leaves the service quietly.

Chapter 10

Lindsey and Samuel are at the statewide Gifted Symposium that summer together. There are cliques of different types of nerds there. Samuel is a Master of Arcane Knowledge, who understands things in a real way, rather than theoretical. One of his heroes is his brother Hal, who dropped out of high school and runs a garage where he fixes motorcycles and other motorized things. Samuel tells people he does not know what he wants to be when he grows up.

Ruth Connors is there as well. She knows she wants to be a poet, and has been writing poetry. Ruth has also become a vegetarian after Susie's death, much to Ruth's mother's dismay. After she ate a whole head of cabbage, she had to be taken to the hospital because she had gastritis. Then she was driven to the symposium.

Lindsey hopes that people at the symposium will not associate her with Susie. She draws a fish instead of writing her last name on her nametag. Lindsey and Samuel had been discreet about their affection during the spring at school, but both of them wear their half-heart pendants.

Both Ruth and Lindsey are "floaters" at camp because they do not belong to any one group. At camp, Ruth decides to eat meat—she knows she can't do it at home because she made a big deal about not eating it. She sees Lindsey in the dining hall and introduces herself. She asks about the fish on Lindsey's nametag. When Ruth says Salmon out loud, Lindsey asks her not to say it. Ruth feels empathy for Lindsey.

Samuel and Lindsey are the only couple at camp. The heat of the summer has brought on their lust. They meet and kiss in a tree. Still, they follow the rules at camp. Ruth writes in her journal that she thinks the couple is going to have sex. Susie likes that Ruth writes everything in her journal, about how she feels connected to Susie and about what it was like to be touched by her soul. Ruth imagines Susie would tell her she's a good poet. Susie can also see that Ruth has a desire for women—Ruth thinks it's not that she wants to have sex with them, but that she wants to hide inside of them.

During the last week of the symposium there is always a project that is contest between the schools. Usually, the contest is to build the best mousetrap. Samuel and Lindsey are already preparing for it by collecting things they need for the trap—small rubber bands from braces, and tin foil. Lindsey does not want to kill the mice. Samuel says Artie is going to contribute tiny coffins. Lindsey mentions that Artie had a crush on Susie and asks if he talks about her. Samuel says that he asks about how Lindsey is doing. Lindsey changes the subject to building a couch for the mice. Samuel doesn't pressure her to talk more about Susie.

Susie does not spend as much time that summer watching earth from the gazebo. At night the shot-putters and javelin throwers in her heaven leave for another part of heaven. She wonders what the other heavens are like. Sometimes, if she wanders too far, she is in the cornfield again and her head throbs. She calls this the lip of her grave. She starts to wonder what heaven means, and why her grandparents aren't there; she wants a place where she feels joy and has no memories. Franny tells her she can only have that if she lets go of watching and caring about what happens on earth.

Ruth comes into Lindsey's dorm and asks to get in bed with her. She tells Lindsey she had a dream about Susie, where Ruth is inside the earth and Susie is walking above in the cornfield; Ruth tries to call to her but he mouth is filled with dirt and Susie can't hear her. Lindsey says she doesn't dream about her. Ruth asks if she misses her, and Lindsey admits that she misses her more than anyone will ever know.

The contest that year is not to make a mousetrap—instead, the kids have to come up with how to commit the perfect murder. Artie wants to break the news to Lindsey before she reads the flier. He approaches her in the breakfast line. She tells him she does not want the little coffins he offered to make for the mice. He tells her the contest is different this year—it's about murder. Samuel comes in and Lindsey asks him what is going on. Samuel confirms what Artie has told her. Lindsey says she is fine and leaves. Artie goes to the table and draws hypodermic needles with embalming fluid dripping out. Susie notes that he is lonely.

Samuel and Lindsey go off to talk. Artie sees Ruth sitting at a picnic table outside. They talk about how each of them found out about Susie's death. Artie's father sat him and his sister down and told them a "little girl" had been killed. Ruth already knew Susie had died but she saw it in the paper that her dad was reading. It starts to rain, and Ruth suggests they just get wet. Artie goes under the table. The rain suddenly stops and the sun comes out. Ruth quietly says that she thinks Susie listens.

All of the students at the symposium now know that Lindsey's sister was murdered. They talked about it, and about the people they knew had died, but they had never known someone who was murdered.

Underneath a boat, Lindsey and Samuel lay together. Samuel gets an erection, and Lindsey tells him she is ready to lose her virginity. Lindsey goes to a place where Susie has never been.

Susie says that in heaven, the game of how to commit the perfect murder is old. Susie always chooses the icicle as her weapon, because it melts away.

Chapter 11

At the Salmon home, Buckley is the only child. Jack gets up early and takes Holiday for a walk, and slows as he passes George Harvey's house. He hopes he will find a clue. He remembers that Ruana Singh told him that if she were Jack, and she were sure of the killer, she would find a quiet way and kill him. Abigail believes in what the police say and not in Jack's theories.

Susie describes the house she grew up in as a box. Mr. Harvey's house is the same as theirs, but more barren. He keeps the house cold. He spends most of his time in the kitchen building dollhouses, in the living room listening to the radio, or sketching blueprints like he did for the hole and the tent. Mr. Harvey has not been bothered about Susie for a few months. He sets alarms so he knows when to open and close the blinds, and when to turn lights on and off. He keeps a routine so no one is suspicious. Late at night, when no one will bother him he counts a few simple things: a wedding ring, a letter sealed in an envelope, the heel of a shoe, a pair of glasses, an eraser the shape of a cartoon character, a small bottle of perfume, a plastic bracelet, Susie's Pennsylvania keystone charm, his mother's amber pendant. He does not remember the names of all of the victims, but Susie knows them all. The heel of the shoe came from a little girl named Claire. Mr. Harvey lured her into the back of a van and took her shoes off; she cried and he did not like the noise, so he went to let her out. But she kept crying. A man banged on the door and asked what he was doing. He pried the heel off one shoe and said he was fixing her shoe. He gave the shoes back but kept the heel. He now rubs in between his fingers like a worry stone.

The darkest place in the house is the crawl space in the basement. When Mr. Harvey's alarm goes off to tell him to shut the blinds, he goes into the basement where no light can leak out. He no longer goes to the crawlspace, but he does sit in an easy chair that faced the space and often falls asleep. Joe Ellis, a boy from the neighborhood, was known for being tough. He had a small dog that one day disappeared, Many other pets in the neighborhood also disappeared. People blamed

Joe Ellis; when he went to the military the disappearances stopped. But Susie discovers that Mr. Harvey was the one killing the pets, whose bones are now in the crawlspace. Susie tries to understand that Mr. Harvey kills animals in order to stop himself from killing a child.

In August Len Fenerman decides he needs to establish boundaries with Jack Salmon. Jack has been calling the precinct about Mr. Harvey non-stop. Len goes to the Salmon house and smokes a cigarette on the porch in the humidity. Lindsey comes out and they chat. She tells him that Buckley has made Len the chief of police in the town he built. Jack takes Len into the kitchen and offers him coffee. Len tells him he has no news; he came to tell him to stop making calls about George Harvey. Lindsey comes in and tells Len that he is giving up. Abigail comes in and Jack sees her look at Len. Jack senses something in her eyes.

That night Jack writes in his journal that Abigail believes Len about George Harvey. Jack has not been doing well at work and has been making a lot of mistakes. Now, the flickering candle distracts him. He turns off his desk lamp and sits in the dark with the candle. He is sitting in his green easy chair, where he often relaxes. When he is about to go to bed, he sees a light outside and it is moving in the direction of the cornfield. Jack believes it is Harvey. He dresses and gets a baseball bat. He goes outside and into the cornfield. Jack remembers what Ruana said about finding a quiet way to kill the man he knows did it. Susie tries to send a warning to him from heaven, to no avail. The person in the cornfield is Clarissa, waiting for Brian. Jack realizes it is not George Harvey.

Brian is late to meet Clarissa. Jack runs into Clarissa in the dark and knocks her down. He screams "Susie!" Brian comes running, his light briefly hits Mr. Harvey, but only Susie sees him. Brian drags Jack off of Clarissa, and then hits him with the baseball bat. Susie knows she can do nothing; all she does is blow out the candle that is flicking in the study window.

Analysis

Both Chapter 8 and Chapter 11 examine Mr. Harvey, his past, and his lifestyle. In Chapter 8, Mr. Harvey dreams of the Church of the Transfiguration, which is an allusion to the transfiguration of Jesus, which is when God put Jesus above Moses and Elijah and when Jesus appeared in radiant glory to three disciples. Also, transfiguration more generally refers to a change in spiritual state. He has this dream after he kills Susie, indicating he feels he is more enlightened after her death. At other times he has dreams that Susie refers to as the "not still" dreams of women and children. These are the dreams where he feels the spirits of the women and children he has killed, and they disturb him—their spirits are "not still."

Susie characterizes Mr. Harvey by giving us a picture of his house, which she describes as barren; even though the house is exactly like her home, his house feels cold while hers feels warm. She also characterizes him by describing his calculated ways—such as setting a timer to tell him when to shut the blinds so he can appear normal. Through Mr. Harvey's thoughts, Susie learns about his parents. Knowing about them and his relationship with them helps her to understand Mr. Harvey. Mr. Harvey thinks of his father's profession as "a builder" which fits into the theme of construction. Mr. Harvey is also a builder in many ways, as he builds dollhouses for a living, and also takes pleasure in building small hideouts, like the one in which he killed Susie.

When Mr. Harvey's mother leaves him and his father, she gives him the amber necklace with a fly locked into place. The fly symbolizes being stuck in time: Mr. Harvey's memory of his mother is of how she looked as she ran away from his father's car. Similarly Susie and his other victims are also locked in time because of their premature deaths. For each woman that is gone, he has one physical memento that represents that woman. Just as Susie's family tries to keep her things, each family member taking representative items for themselves, Mr. Harvey uses objects to represent absence.

In Chapter 9, Susie states that Grandma Lynn brings the light back into the Salmon household, which is emblematic of her support as she helps them to survive their grief. The make-up that Lynn applies on Lindsey's face is a marker of adulthood for her—but as an adult she also has responsibility and independence. Before the memorial service, Lindsey worries that she has forgotten what Susie looked like, emphasizing the theme of memory—it's the only place Susie "lives" which makes it all the more important for Lindsey. The memorial service is an acknowledgment of Susie's physical absence from their lives. Her absence is what has kept the family members preoccupied yet it is not very often discussed between them. Ray also says goodbye to Susie that day, but not at the memorial service. Instead he chooses to figuratively bury Susie's picture in the volume of Indian poetry. Thus he feels he has set her free, and finds his own way of surviving grief and letting her go; he also realizes that Susie is in his relationship with Ruth, that she does not really exist in the picture he has of her. At Susie's memorial service, her body is not present; Susie remembers a service she went to for Mrs. Utemeyer where her body was present. However, Mrs. Utemeyer's body has an absence of soul. Just as the picture is not Susie, the body is not Mrs. Utemeyer.

Lindsey's move toward becoming an adult is continued when Lindsey looses her virginity to Samuel. Susie realizes that Lindsey is growing up in a way that Susie was never able to because Lindsey's sex brings her to a place Susie did not go. Susie uses a metaphor to describe the difference: the "walls" of her sex had horror and blood, while the walls of Lindsey's have windows. We are reminded of the tone set by the rape in the first chapter. For Susie, all sex she sees on Earth is colored by her experience with Mr. Harvey.

Right before Lindsey's sex scene, Susie watches Artie, a loner from her school. While watching him she comments "Lonely… on earth as it is in heaven." Susie empathizes with Artie because she too feels isolated in heaven. He feels isolated because the nerds at the gifted symposium formed cliques that leave some on the outside. When Jack goes into the cornfield seeking revenge, we are reminded of Susie's isolation from Earth. Susie tries to push on the Inbetween to warn Jack but is not able to help him. Susie isolated in her world and Jack in his.

Analysis

Summary and Analysis of Chapters 12-14

Chapter 12

Susie watches her father in the hospital. The story told about him is that he is crazy with grief and was seeking revenge. He has to have his kneecap replaced. The surgeon is very patient; he is Jack's age and has children of his own.

Abigail, Lindsey and Buckley are awakened by the sound of sirens. Abigail tells Lindsey to get her father and they discover he is not there. Abigail is angry because she realizes that Jack must have gone after Harvey. Lindsey wants to help him but Abigail does not want her to. Lindsey has no choice; she takes Buckley up to her room to go back to sleep. Abigail gets a call from the police that Jack has been hit by a baseball bat. Lindsey stays at home while Abigail goes to the hospital.

Lindsey calls Nate's mother to get Buckley. Then she calls Samuel so Hal can pick her up on his motorcycle and take her to the hospital. Abigail is not in the room when Lindsey arrives. Hal tells Lindsey he will wait outside in case she needs a ride. Lindsey sings a song to her father that he used to sing to his daughters before Buckley was born. Jack is completely unconscious and unaware of his life and his surroundings. In heaven Franny tells Susie that when the dead are done with the living, the living can move on. Susie wants to know what the dead do, but Franny won't answer.

Len Fenerman comes to the hospital because Abigail requested him. At the hospital Abigail is pacing and she is still wearing her nightgown and raincoat, but she has applied red lipstick. Len arrives and Abigail is relieved. Len suggests they talk in the visitors' area. Len fills Abigail in on what happened in the cornfield. Len and Abigail go to a balcony to smoke cigarettes. Abigail asks Len how his wife died. He tells her she committed suicide. Susie is struck by the way her mother looks smoking the cigarette—she looks like the mother Susie photographed, the Abigail who never had children. She asks why his wife killed herself and Len tells her he doesn't know but that the question preoccupies him when he is not thinking about Susie's murder. Abigail smiles when he says "your daughter's murder" because no one in the neighborhood ever talks about it directly. She has him repeat the phrase, and then she kisses him.

Susie was always aware that her mother was irresistible, especially when in need. But her father had always been the one who could make her let go and make her laugh. When Lindsey and Susie were little, their father would come home from work early on Thursdays and that was Mommy and Daddy time. Abigail would have them bathe early, and tell them stories from Greek mythology. Abigail has a master's in English, and Susie felt like her birth prevented her mother from doing what she wanted to do. After the bath she would dry them both as they chattered and then put them down for a nap. Susie and Abigail tucked Lindsey in together and then Abigail would tuck Susie in and confide in her. Abigail was lonely and Susie, as the oldest, was her only friend. One day she asked Susie if she knows who Persephone was. Susie did not answer because she has learned that bath time is when she is allowed to talk, but when they are in her room it is her mother's turn to talk. She told her all about Persephone while Susie fell asleep. Sometimes Susie was awoken by laughter and the sounds of love-making; Susie would pretend they were all in a ship with the ocean all around them.

Everything shifted for Abigail when she got pregnant with Buckley. She stopped reading the novels she was always so fond of and began replacing them with books on parenting, cooking, and gardening. She sealed away the mysterious mother. But even though she had bottled up that part of her, she was still needy, and this came out in her kiss with Len. He resists, but she wants him to kiss her and touch her so she can forget.

Susie notes that she used to watch her mother ride the lawn mower, and remembers how she used to whistle when she made her tea and how her face would light up when Jack brought her marigolds. With just Jack, she was in love, but with her children she grew away while Jack grew closer to them.

Abigail passes Hal as she goes back to Jack's room. He stops her to tell her Lindsey is in there. Abigail realizes she needs to gather herself together, which was Hal's purpose in stopping her. Lindsey has fallen asleep while holding her father's hand. Susie watches the three of them in the room together. She remembers playing hide-and-seek with her mother when she was little, trying to win her approval. She decides now that she will not divide them in her heart.

Susie and Holly sometimes watch the souls coming up from hospitals when they cannot sleep at night. Franny tells Susie when she first arrives that she still loves to watch them. When Susie first started to watch them, she felt them before she saw them, and they looked like tiny sparks, or fireflies. Franny compares them to snowflakes—each one is different but from where they are they all look the same.

Chapter 13

When Lindsey returns to school in the fall she is known as the daughter of the nutcase, which she finds very hurtful because she knows it is not true. Clarissa and Brian are in high school and they use the incident to make them cool. Clarissa has lost her virginity to Brian and Susie notes that everyone she knows is growing up. Buckley goes to kindergarten that year and has a crush on his teacher, Miss Koekle. He is set apart from the other children because of Susie's death.

No one goes inside the Salmon house except for family. Jack's leg will always be stiff but he should be able to walk again. Buckley asks a lot of questions about his father's fake knee. He brings reports of what his father says and of kindergarten to his mother, who listens and nods. She becomes absorbed in the small tasks of being a mother, cutting vegetables, washing lunchboxes, folding clothes, etc. When Buckley talks to her she pays attention for a few minutes and then lets her mind wander and thinks of Len.

By November, Jack can hobble, and Buckley eggs him on. The one year anniversary of Susie's death is approaching. Jack has taken an extended sick leave from his firm; everyone there treats him differently now. He no longer pursues Mr. Harvey or mentions him to Abigail. He apologizes for this to Susie in his journal. He sets his return to the firm for December 2nd, right before the anniversary. He notices that Abigail is pulling away. Jack decides he will build back his strength and pursue Mr. Harvey.

Grandma Lynn is due for a Thanksgiving visit. Lindsey has been keeping up a beauty regime prescribed by her. Abigail considers beautifying for Len, but realizes she is not in love with him, that she wants to use him to forget. Two weeks before Thanksgiving Jack decides to try and give Buckley a piggyback to return to father-child normalcy. The piggyback is successful, and they run up the stairs and find Lindsey shaving her legs in the bathroom. Jack tells her she is too young to shave her legs. Jack sends Buckley to his room and then offers to get Lindsey a fresh blade. He gives her tips on how to shave. Lindsey offers to let him stay. Jack mentions they never talk about Susie—Lindsey says it is because she is everywhere. She asks him if he still thinks George Harvey did it and he says he does. She asks why Len does not arrest him, but Jack explains that it is not that simple; there is no evidence, nothing to link Harvey to Susie. They wish they could find her body.

The make-up Lindsey wears does not completely disguise the fact that her eyes look like Susie's. Lindsey realizes that talking about finding evidence makes her father see her as Lindsey instead of a combination of his two daughters. Lindsey suggests they need to get into Harvey's house. Jack hesitates and tells her that is illegal—but Lindsey knows he needs someone to do it for him.

Grandma Lynn arrives on the Monday before Thanksgiving. She notices something different in Abigail's eyes. Lynn offers to help Abigail clean up, which is very rare. Abigail refuses but Lynn insists. They do it in silence. Then Lynn suggests they go for a walk because she knows something is going on with Abigail. On the walk Lynn tells Abigail that her father had a long-term affair with another woman. Abigail tells her she is not sure why she is telling her this. Lynn takes her hand; the two of them have never been affectionate, so the action is awkward. Lynn admits that Susie's death helped her mourn her own husband's death, which she never did properly. Abigail tells Lynn she resents her for that. Lynn is glad for the nugget of truth. Abigail admits she has always felt alone. Lynn asks Abigail to stop seeing the man she is seeing; Abigail says she is not seeing anyone, and asks if she could use her father's cabin if she needs to get away. Abigail suggests they walk past George Harvey's house. Then they smell foreign cigarettes; Abigail goes off in pursuit of them, and Lynn heads home. Abigail finds Ruana Singh smoking. Ruana is not startled by Abigail; she calls her Mrs. Salmon and tells her she is glad to see her. Dr.

Singh is having a party and Ruana has discreetly stepped out to smoke. Ruana comments that they live in a weird place. Abigail asks for a cigarette and asks Ruana to call her Abigail. Ray can smell the cigarettes from his room and wonders what Abigail is doing outside with his mother. He also wonders if things would have been different if he had kissed Susie on the scaffolding.

Lynn continues on the route planned by Abigail. When she passes George Harvey's house she feels that it radiates malevolence. She decides she should have sympathy for Abigail because she is living inside of a figurative ground zero. She will offer her the keys to the cabin so she can use them anytime.

That night Abigail has a wonderful dream; she dreams she is in India. A young girl is led to a pyre and wrapped and burned alive. The bright fire brings Abigail to bliss; before the girl was burned her body had been clean and whole.

Chapter 14

Lindsey watches George Harvey's house while she is running with the soccer team. Samuel runs with her; he is good at running but not at soccer. Since he runs ahead to set the pace, he does not notice her scoping out Harvey's house. But Harvey notices and it makes him itch. This has happened to him before, where only a girl's family will suspect him. He leaves the house daily for an hour or two to pick up supplies and go for a walk in Valley Forge Park. Sometimes he runs into field trips there, and when the teachers give him questioning stares he gives them a line about how he used to take his kids there or that he met his wife there. He talks about his victims as if they were his wives. He uses whichever one is on his mind at the time. Once a heavy woman converses with him; he imagines her dead in his basement. After that he no longer talks to anyone at the park.

On November 26th, 1974 Lindsey sees Mr. Harvey leave his house while she is running with her team. She feigns a cramp and waits until the boys have all passed her. She breaks the glass in the basement window in order to get in. Lindsey thinks of Samuel and how he will wait for her. She wonders how long he will wait. She has not told anyone about what she was doing. Lindsey wanted to go through the rooms methodically to find clues. Mr. Harvey's house is laid out the same as theirs but it has no warmth. She is flooded with memories from childhood, of chasing Susie, of Susie giving Buckley piggybacks, of Susie putting the star on the Christmas tree, and more—about Holiday, about Easter. She sees Susie darting into the other room. She is a child running ahead of her. Susie realizes she may be pushing too hard on the Inbetween and she might hurt her instead of helping. She notes that all of Harvey's victims are present in the house, and calls their names: Jackie Meyer, Flora Hernandez, Leah Fox, Sophie Cichetti, Leidia Johnson, Wendy Richter. Then Susie pays attention to Lindsey again. Lindsey goes upstairs and sees Harvey's sketchbook. At the same time, Harvey pulls into the drive-way. Lindsey finds a sketch of the hole he had made in Stolfuz cornfield, where he killed Susie. She rips the page out and escapes out the window, but not before Harvey sees her.

When Lindsey comes home everyone is there, including Grandma Lynn and Samuel. Lindsey only speaks to her father, and gives him what she has found. He asks if she believes him now, and she says she does. Abigail is irritated and states she is going to pick up Buckley. Jack places a call to the police station.

Susie is grateful her sister was able to escape unharmed. Franny gives Susie a map to a field she has seen but never explored. Susie goes there and meets a little girl who also knows Franny. She introduces herself as Flora Hernandez, and Susie introduces herself as well and begins to cry at knowing another girl he killed. Flora tells her the other will arrive soon.

Analysis

The theme of guilt and responsibility is prevalent in these chapters. Jack's decision to venture into the cornfield to pursue who he thought was Mr. Harvey shows his feeling of responsibility to avenge Susie's death. His injuries weaken him—he can only hobble. He has a physical loss of strength that is symbolizes the physical and emotional loss of Susie. But his recovery from his injury parallels his survival of grief. With his recovery he is more able to be a father to Buckley, giving him a piggyback ride. He is also able to be a there for Lindsey and stops seeing Susie in Lindsey, seeing her at last as her own person.

Meanwhile, Abigail is more and more mentally and emotionally absent from the family. Her mental and emotional absence is her way of removing herself from the pain. Abigail's distance from her family is emphasized when Jack finds Lindsey shaving her legs and he is the one who gives her tips on how to shave, rather than her mother. With Susie's death, the roles in the family are no longer as clear—Lindsey acts as a parent to Buckley and to her father, and Jack is a "mother" to Lindsey in this situation. Jack also acts as Lindsey's child in many ways, since Lindsey feels the responsibility to take care of him. When she speaks to him in the bathroom she wants to help her father prove that George Harvey is her sister's murderer; she is taking care of him because she knows he cannot do it himself.

Although Abigail is pulling away from her family now, Susie remembers when her mother used to bathe her and Lindsey when they were little, before Buckley was born. During this time she was not as distant from her family because she still allowed her true self to shine through. When Abigail is telling stories, the author includes an intertextual reference to Greek mythology. Persephone was captured by Hades and brought to the underworld to be the queen. While she was there she ate pomegranate seeds, which caused her to have to commit part of her year to the underworld. This story is a loose parallel to Abigail, who is trapped by motherhood and is thus obligated to be a mother even though that is not the "world" she wants to be in. Like Persephone, she still spends part of her time as the true Abigail, who loves literature and is in love with Jack.

While Susie and Lindsey were the first products of her and Jack's love, and were thus the initial "seeds" that made her obligated to a life as a mother, Buckley's birth makes her completely resign herself to motherhood. Sebold uses the metaphor to describe how Abigail "bottled" the mysterious part of her when she had Buckley; the metaphor demonstrates how Abigail has contained her real self for many years because she believed being a mother was more important. This part of her comes out in her affair with Len. She also uses the affair as a way of filling the Susie's absence. The affair signifies the completion of her psychological absence from her family. The dream Abigail has at the end of Chapter 13 is representative of her desire to escape. The wholeness of the girl's body in the dream is a wistful reminder of what she does not have with Susie—she has nothing to burn, no body to get rid of, yet she has an emotional burden that she wants to be free from.

Isolation is another prevalent theme in these chapters. After Jack's incident in the cornfield, the Salmons are the only ones who go inside their house. They have isolated themselves from the neighborhood and from any outside influences. The implication is that the neighborhood also seems to think they need to be left alone in order to recover from the incident and from Susie's death as the one-year anniversary approaches. Lynn thinks of the household as a "ground zero"—metaphorically, Susie's death was an explosion. Lynn realizes this because Abigail admits to her mother how alone she is; she is the most cut off of all of the family members in the house. She connects to Ruana as another isolated mother.

The Salmon children are isolated as well. Buckley is set apart from the other children at school by his teacher, who gives him special treatment. Lindsey decides to go to Mr. Harvey's house alone to investigate. While there, Susie refers back to the title of her paper on Othello, turned in right before her death "The Ostracized: One Man Alone." The "ostracized" is Lindsey, as she excludes herself from the soccer run to go on this mission, alone. Her action parallels Mr. Harvey, because he too has separated himself from society and chooses to live his life alone. While she is at Mr. Harvey's house, she thinks of photographs that were taken of her and Susie on special occasions; she remembers that they always turn out fuzzy and she doesn't feel they capture the moments when they were sisters. Here, Lindsey notes the lack of power a photograph has to truly convey a relationship between two people. Being at Mr. Harvey's house, Susie is no longer isolated because she can see that parts of all his other victims are there too. The author uses exposition to list off Mr. Harvey's other victims. Chapter 14 ends with Susie meeting all of the other victims in heaven and having the opportunity to tell her story; she feels that this is the solution to her longing and her pain—which related to the theme of finding ways to "survive" the grief of her death.

Summary and Analysis of Chapters 15, 16 & Snapshots

Chapter 15

George Harvey remembers trips he used to take with his mother when he was eight. They would go into town and steal things, thinking of themselves as scavengers. When they were caught Harvey felt fear, and he could sense when they were going to be caught. His mother began making him hide the stolen items on his body, which she found thrilling. He felt free and warm then. Once when they are passing a gravesite his mother told him that it's good to look past the dead, and they take some charms and the flowers from a grave. Harvey senses they are doing something wrong. They sleep together in the truck that night and are awoken by three drunken men staring at his mother. She moves slowly and has Harvey turn the key to the truck so they can escape. Harvey realizes living as a child or as a woman are the two worst things to be.

George Harvey watches Lindsey run away. He then hides the knife in a hole in the basement, and he wraps up all of the trinkets, minus Susie's Pennsylvania keystone, and puts them deep in the foundation. He has already buried the book of sonnets that he kept from the murder scene. He then calls the police and reports his home has been broken into.

When Jack calls the station he asks for Len Fenerman but he cannot be found. He is informed that two uniforms have already gone to Harvey's house. Mr. Harvey lets the police search his house, which impresses them. They believe he is sincere in his sympathy for the Salmons. They see the dollhouses that he builds and they ask him about them. They know about the stolen drawing, but Harvey does not mention it to them. They ask him about it, he reacts by showing the police a similar drawing and explaining that he had obsessed over how it had happened, and had come up with that structure. They asked why he had not shown it to the police, and he says he did not want to meddle. They tell him Len will probably want to see the sketch tomorrow.

Meanwhile, after Abigail picks up Buckley she calls Len from a pay phone and asks him to meet her at the mall. She drops Buckley off at the play circle and he is excited to be there. Inside a store, Len brushes by her and heads out of the store. She follows him. He unlocks a door and takes her into the inner workings of the mall. She follows him to the end of the corridor into a large room full of metal tanks and drums. She feels like she is inside a heart, and thinks of Jack when the doctor told him he had risk of heart failure. Len watches Abigail as she finds him—he sees the need in her eyes. He feels bad for the family but he cannot resist her eyes. He reaches out and touches her. They kiss. They do not know that Mr. Harvey is packing his belongings. The others wait at home, Lindsey and Samuel dressed and lying on her bed, Grandma Lynn doing shots, Jack watching the phone. Len and Abigail undress.

At home, Samuel kisses Lindsey's neck and thinks to himself that he never wants to leave her. Abigail undresses completely—she has the adult body Susie will never have. Mr. Harvey leaves his house while Abigail commits adultery.

Chapter 16

Dr. Singh is late for dinner, and Ruana goes about her routine of stretching. She knows he is kept late by ambition rather than by a woman. She no longer has ambition after she injured herself dancing. Still, she keeps herself in good shape. She can hear noises from the neighborhood, but then they are drowned out by Ray's loud music. The doorbell rings and she lets Ruth Connors in.

Ruth has decided she wants to do something to mark the anniversary of Susie's death. She sees candles at the grocery store and knows that Ray will come with her to mark the anniversary. Ray and Ruth have begun to kiss as an experiment. Neither of them feel anything, and Ruth thinks she is gay, but they decide to keep trying anyway. Now Ruth finds Ray dancing in his room. A drawing Ruth did of Susie hangs over Ray's bed. She asks him to go light the candles in the cornfield with her. She offers to kiss him for a while, and Ray has secretly begun to like this. They kiss until Ruth swears and says she thinks she feels something.

Ruth and Ray arrive at the cornfield holding hands. Samuel and Hal Heckler are already there. There are daffodils on the ground that were already there when Samuel and Hal arrived. Mrs. Stead joins them. Grace Tarking sees and calls a few others to join. The Gilberts come and join. By the time it is completely dark, Susie notes that almost everyone she has ever known is in the cornfield with candles. Rumors of George Harvey's guilt had begun to spread, and people wondered if it was true. Susie buzzes with heat and energy in heaven as she watches the people at the vigil. No one calls the Salmons; they are left undisturbed.

Lindsey realizes they are having a ceremony for Susie. Abigail is not interested because she is "done" with that. She tells Lindsey she wants to be more than a mother. Lindsey asks her if she is going to leave. She lies and promises she won't. She holds Lindsey and tells her she is helping keep her father alive. Jack pulls into the driveway. She then tells Lindsey to get her father.

Jack agrees to go, and they decide to bring Buckley and not to protect him from Susie's death anymore. Lindsey takes Buckley upstairs to get dressed. He tells her he sees Susie. She hugs him and tells him she'll always be there for him. Abigail continues to read her Moliere book, and goes into the dining room where Jack will not see her. Ruth sees the Salmons approaching and tells Ray to go help Jack. Jack realizes Susie was loved by people he doesn't recognize. He tells Mr. O'Dwyer that Susie used to listen to him sing on summer nights, and asks him to sing a song for them; he sings and everyone joins in.

Susie remembers the summer nights when she listened to Mr. O'Dwyer. Sometimes, she would smell a thunderstorm coming. She'd change into a cotton nightgown and go out onto the back porch. Her mother would stand and watch, telling her she'd catch cold, but then telling her she looked invincible. Susie would agree.

Snapshots

When Lindsey was given her camera she took so many pictures that she had to pick which rolls she wanted developed and which ones she did not. She loved that photography made it seem like she had found a way to stop time.

In the summer of 1975 Abigail asks Jack if he ever made love in the ocean. He says no. She asks him to pretend they are making love in the ocean and that he will not see her again for a long time. She leaves the next day for her father's cabin in New Hampshire.

That summer, the neighbors leave food on the doorstep for the Salmons. Jack's favorite is Ruana's apple pie. In the fall Grandma Lynn calls and tells Jack she is coming to stay. Jack needs help with the children and she offers it. He realizes they will have to put her in Susie's room.

December 1975 marks a year since George Harvey left and there is no sign of him. Local storeowners still keep a sketch of him in the window. Lindsey asks Hal to take her to the police station so she can see what they are doing. When she is there she sees her mother's scarf on Len's desk; she knows it is her mother's because it is Chinese red, a bright red that her mother frequently wears. She asks Len why he has it. He makes up an excuse. Hal tells her they should go. Lindsey cries in disbelief to Samuel later.

At seven years old Buckley decides to make a fort that Susie always promised she would make with him. Jack cannot bring himself to help because it reminds him of building the tent with Mr. Harvey. Buckley uses whatever he can find to make walls, and Lindsey, Samuel and Hal help him drag boulders to use. Hal gives Buckley corrugated tin to use as a roof. Jack shuts out the noise by keeping his den window closed. When the fort is finished Jack cannot see his son out the window. Buckley lets in enough light to see his comic books. He misses Susie at odd moments; he also wishes his family would play with him like they used to, without worry behind their eyes. He does not allow himself to miss his mother. Buckley writes a story where a boy goes into a hole and never comes out. Jack doesn't notice it but Buckley knows there is something wrong with the story, so he hides it in the box spring in Susie's old bed.

In the fall of 1976 Len Fenerman visits a safe that contains evidence from Susie's case. All they found in Mr. Harvey's house were the bones of the animals. They searched the field again and found an old coke bottle with Harvey's prints and Susie's prints, linking them. But he cannot find Harvey. Len sees the jingle bell hat and remembers how Abigail collapsed when he gave it to her. He wonders when it was that he fell in love with her; Susie knows it was when he watched her draw on butcher paper in crayon. Susie feels bad for him, because he feels guilty that he missed his chance at catching George Harvey when he was with Abigail at the mall. Len takes all of the photos of the unsolved cases out of his wallet and writes "gone" on the back of them. He does not know that in Connecticut on September 10, 1976 a hunter found Susie's Pennsylvania keystone charm alongside a grave that had been dug up by a bear, and the bones of child's foot were exposed.

After one winter in New Hampshire Abigail decides to drive to California to work in the wineries. She realizes that sex is not the way out. On her drive across the country she sends Lindsey and Buckley postcards of the places she stops. She buys herself a bottle of champagne for her arrival in California. She remembers the New Year's Eve that all of the family had stayed up until midnight. The strike of midnight was anti-climatic. Jack lifted up Buckley and sang Auld Lang Syne. When Buckley asks what it means, Abigail gets lost in her own world.

When Abigail reaches the beach she parks the car and walks along the cliffs. Abigail thinks of the books she read in college. Abigail wants to reach the waves, so she climbs down the cliffs. Susie worries she will slip. Abigail walks along the beach; she sees a baby sitting alone by the water. Soon she realizes that the baby is being photographed and she laughs. Abigail thinks about how the waves could sweep the baby away and none of the adults could do anything. Later that week she gets a job at Krusoe Winery. She writes to Lindsey and Buckley. On her days off she goes to the nearby towns of Santa Rosa and Sausilito, but she finds that even in unfamiliar places she cannot escape her grief.

Jack organizes a yearly memorial for Susie. Each year fewer people come. Students at the high school now only know her as a name; saying her name out loud simultaneously resurrects her and buries her, she is just the Murdered. Only a few, like Mr. Botte, remember her as a real girl.

Ray Singh has grown into an attractive seventeen year-old, not quite a man yet. Susie feels a longing for him. Ray often reads his favorite book, Gray's Anatomy, and finds the parts on his own body. He goes to Penn for college. Susie worries his head is filled with too much memorization and not enough room for his friendship with Ruth or his love for his mother and his memory of Susie. Ruana packs the book of Indian poetry containing Susie's picture, and when he unpacks at school her picture falls out; he cannot avoid seeing the lips he kissed.

On graduation day Ruth and Ray are already gone. Ruth moves to New York City. Ray graduated early. At the Salmon house, Grandma Lynn introduces Buckley to gardening.

Abigail calls the house from California on occasion. In one conversation in 1977, Jack tells her they miss her. She says she knows. He asks her about teaching, which was what she wanted to do. She says plans change.

In New York Ruth lives in a closet sized room on the Lower East Side. She wears all black. She scans the streets for places women have been murdered.

Ray reads about death in his textbook and how the visions people see are often the result of strokes. He wonders if a soul will ever touch him like Susie touched Ruth.

Mr. Harvey lives up and down the Northeast corridor, often camping. He still likes to drive to the Salmons' development in early morning or late night when no one will notice. He knows how to pick wild mushrooms; one night in Valley Forge Park he finds novice campers dead from eating poisonous mushrooms and he takes their valuables.

Buckley only lets Hal, Nate and Holiday into his fort. When he is ten Hal encourages him to waterproof it so that it doesn't get puddles. Grandma Lynn gets excited when Hal comes over and dresses up and makes muffins. Jack teases her.

In December 1981 Len gets a call from Delaware that links a 1976 Connecticut murder to Susie's murder because of the Pennsylvania keystone charm. The body in Connecticut has teeth so they ask for Susie's dental records. Len does not call the Salmons. He wants the case to remain closed.

Since Hal had heard of the drawing Lindsey found, he tries to track George Harvey down through his biker network. One day he meets Ralph Cichetti, who says he thinks his mother was killed by her boarder. Cichetti tells Hal the man built dollhouses, and Hal makes a call to Len.

Years pass and Susie still watches her family and friends. She always ends her day watching her father in his den. She can trace how all of the people she watches are connected by her death. One night at Evensong, Susie sees Holiday, who had lived to old age on earth; he is so happy to see her he knocks her down.

Analysis

Chapter 15 opens with more exposition on Mr. Harvey's childhood, as Susie attempts to understand where Mr. Harvey comes from and why he is this way. His mother's love is free and warm but unpredictable; the freedom is countered by the fear he feels when they get caught stealing, a feeling in his stomach that is compared in simile to "eggs being folded in a bowl." In Susie's previous description of Mr. Harvey's house, she describes it as cold; instead of the unpredictable warmth of love, Mr. Harvey chose the coldness of killing and being alone. His mother teaches him that sometimes he needs to look past the dead to take their trinkets. At the time he felt it was wrong, but the grown-up Mr. Harvey now takes the keepsakes from his victims. Sebold fleshes out Harvey's character by exposing the places where Mr. Harvey used to have feelings and morals, and also where he learned to be unfeeling.

The fear Mr. Harvey has of getting caught stealing with his mother is paralleled by his fear when he sees Lindsey escaping from his home.

Besides Lindsey's escape from Mr. Harvey's house, there are two other escapes that run parallel in Chapter 15: Abigail escapes her pain through adultery, and Mr. Harvey escapes from being caught for Susie's murder. However, neither Abigail nor Mr. Harvey truly escape from what they are running from—both of them still have the guilt of knowing they did something wrong. While Abigail is following Len through the inner working of the mall, she feels like she is inside her heart, but then she is reminded of Jack's heart—alluding to the fact that she is inside his heart as well, and that their hearts are in some ways the same.

By escaping, both Abigail and Mr. Harvey attempt to move on from Susie's death. Throughout these chapters, many of the characters find their own ways of moving on and letting go of Susie, building on the theme of surviving grief. Ruth and Ray's relationship progresses and becomes sexual. At first the kissing was an attempt to imagine Susie as alive, but as they continued to do it they began to have their own feelings about each other and Susie is no longer constantly present in their relationship. In Snapshots Susie notes that Ray is growing up and becoming handsome; in heaven Susie feels an attraction to him that is also maturing. Her maturation is symbolized by her picture, in which Ray sees the lips he had once kissed, thus sexualizing the picture and foreshadowing the consummation of their relationship later in the book.

All of the people who ever knew Susie are also moving on from her death, as demonstrated by the impromptu memorial in the cornfield. Seeing the people celebrating her memory, Susie "buzzed with heat and energy" because she lives in the memories of others, so when they commemorate her she feels more alive. But she also notices that everyone is saying goodbye to her, never to think of her again. The Salmon house has been isolated up to this point, and the author uses a simile to describe this isolation, saying there is an invisible barrier like a layer of clear ice. However, Abigail does not leave the house, and instead focuses on her desire to be more than a mother. She goes back to her "mysterious" self by pulling out her old college books; she reads Moliere and distances herself from her family and from Susie. Her psychological absence from the family is coming to a climax—she physically leaves the family soon afterwards.

In the chapter Snaphots, Susie fast-forwards through the lives of her family, friends, Len and George Harvey, showing how time passing has helped them to build anew in her absence. The snapshots of the title also refer to the photographs Susie has in her mind of all the things she watches; she believes that as long as she is watching, those moments are not lost. Susie explains that she liked photography because it allowed her to capture a moment in time, a moment that is now gone forever. In heaven, Susie continues to capture the moments where she exists in people's memories.

In Snapshots, characters continue to survive their grief and their guilt over losing Susie. Len keeps all of the evidence from Susie's case in a "safety box"—a parallel to the safe that Susie is in in the sinkhole. Len continues to feel guilty, but he is also able to let go of the dead, shown in his writing "gone" on the backs of all of the pictures of unsolved cases. Buckley builds a fort for Susie, furthering the theme of construction because he is building anew after Susie is gone. Buckley also takes up gardening, showing his growth symbolically. Lynn comes to live with the family and sleeps in Susie's old room—by putting a new occupant in Susie's room, Jack shows he is beginning to accept that she is not coming back. Ruth and Ray both move off to new places, away from the town, but Susie still comes to their minds on occasion. On Abigail's trip to California, she remembers the song sung on New Year's Eve the time when the whole family celebrated together. The lyrics "old acquaintance be forgot and never brought to mind" are representative of leaving behind the old and bringing in the new, which is what happens at New Year's. The same is happening now for Susie's family and friends and Len.

Summary and Analysis of Chapters 17-20

Chapter 17

Lindsey and Samuel both graduate from college at Temple University. They are riding back to the Salmon house on Samuel's motorcycle when it starts to rain. They have to pull over when they are eight miles away from the house. They wheel the bike under some trees. They are dressed in leather; Hal had insisted that Lindsey get some for riding. Both of them take off their helmets; they have matching short spiky haircuts. The rain makes Lindsey's mascara run, Samuel wishes her a happy graduation and kisses her. Susie has always known that Samuel would be Lindsey's one and only ever since he kissed her on the Christmas after Susie's death. The couple decides to find the deepest part of the underbrush. They come upon a large abandoned house. They go inside to keep dry. They explore the house. Samuel is fascinated by the carpentry. Samuel comments that you could wall someone into a place like this. They both have an awkward silence where they think of Susie, and where she is. Susie anticipates these moments, but usually no one brings her up anymore. But because of the occasion of graduation, Lindsey does think about her a little longer than usual. Samuel climbs the stairs and tells Lindsey that he wants the house. Susie leaves them as they unzip their leather.

At home, Jack sits in his den. He holds the snow globe on his desk, shakes it, and watches the Penguin disappear and reappear in the falling snow. Hal had already come back to the house on his bike, and Jack is worried something happened to Lindsey and Samuel. Jack now has a slower reaction time than he did previously. Buckley comes into the den to comfort his father. Jack tells him that he looked good in his suit. Buckley, at thirteen, is glad to hear this—he is in an awkward stage between boy and man, but he had wanted to wear the suit for the graduation. Buckley tells Jack that Hal and Grandma Lynn are waiting downstairs.

That fall Jack developed the last roll of film that Susie kept in the box of film to hold back. At the time, he told Susie that her artistic shots were foolhardy. Yet, one of the best portraits of him is one that she took close up at an angle. He does not know what order the rolls go in. There are lots of pictures of Holiday and Susie's feet in the grass. There is one roll that consists of portraits of Abigail. Looking at these photos, Jack falls in love with her all over again. In one series of pictures, Susie captures her mother's expressions as her father arrives home from work. As he pulls in the driveway she looks anxious, and as he comes in she starts to put on a mask of distance, and by the time he kisses her on the cheek she has put the entire mask on. Jack asks himself if he did that to her.

Lindsey points out that the lightning has stopped. The couple has just finished making love. Samuel tells Lindsey he loves her, he wants to marry her and he wants to live in this house. Lindsey hesitates, asking who will support them, and then says yes. Susie is very happy for them. Lindsey is so happy she is crying, and Samuel holds her. Then she realizes that her father will be worried. They decide to run the eight miles back to the house wearing only their underwear and t-shirts. They get completely soaked by the cars passing them. Susie realizes that Lindsey is neither running away from her or toward her; she has a wound that has been slowly closing over eight years and forming a scar.

At home, Hal is helping Lynn by cutting brownies. The couple appears at the door soaked. Jack tells them he was so worried and he gets them blankets and starts a fire in the fireplace. While they sit by the fire they tell the story of getting caught in the rain and finding the house. Samuel tells Jack that they ran back for him because Lindsey was worried. Both of Jack's surviving children live to make sure they do not hurt their fragile father. Buckley, Lynn and Hal leave the room to get the brownies. While they are gone Hal tells Jack that he proposed to Lindsey. As everyone comes back in, Lindsey asks him what he thinks, and he tells Samuel he is happy to have him as his son-in-law. Everyone in the room is elated, and they drink the champagne that they got for the graduation. Buckley sees Susie appear under the colonial clock. She has strings coming out from all around her; she is there for a moment and then she is gone.

Over the years Susie sometimes gets tired of watching. She will instead sit in the back of trains as they come in and out of Philadelphia. She listens to the people on the trains. She also listens to the other souls who watch their loved ones on earth. They are constantly talking to the people they watch and sometimes listening to them talk is overwhelming, especially when the train is traveling between stations. Susie also watches women hang and collect clothes from clotheslines. She thinks of the times when her mother would warn her and Lindsey not to get peanut butter on the sheets, and about the time Abigail found lemon candy spots on one of their father's shirts. After the graduation, Susie rides the trains until she can only think of the times when she would hold the ship in the bottle while her father burned away the strings; then, the whole world in the bottle depended on her.

Chapter 18

In New York, Ruth finds out from her father that developers are going to close up the sinkhole. Ruth plans on going back to see the sinkhole before it is closed up. Ruth keeps a lot secret in New York, like her fascination with the sinkhole; she also does not talk about her experience with Susie in the parking lot. Instead she writes in her journal. Even though Ruth no longer looks haunted, she still has a look in her eye like she is on the lookout for something. Patrons at the bar she works at tell her she has beautiful hair, or hands, or legs, but never mention her eyes. After the phone call Ruth dresses in all black clothes, most of them dirty from bartending. She only notices the stains once she is in the sunshine. The only person Ruth keeps in touch with from high school is Ray. While still at high school she found out that Lindsey's mother left, and she tried to offer her support to Lindsey as best she could without ruining Lindsey's reputation, since Ruth was known as a freak. Ruth knows when she goes back she will take Ray with her to see the sinkhole.

Often when Ruth is walking the city she will stop in places that she is certain a woman has been killed, and then write the place in her journal later. For this reason, Ruth becomes a celebrity in heaven, and women line up to find out if Ruth has found where they were killed. Susie watches Ruth more closely, and she finds the moments Ruth has painful and amazing. Ruth will stop and get an image in her mind, sometimes a flash, and sometimes an entire scenario. The people in heaven feel Ruth is doing important work for them.

The day after the graduation, Susie watches Ruth as she walks to Central Park and sits in Sheep Meadow. Ruth prefers to go to places that people consider safe. Ruth sits by the zoo and takes out her notebook. While in New York she realized that it is better to look like she is doing something when she is staring out into space. Ruth sees a girl stray from her nanny, and is about to call out to her when the nanny wakes. Ruth thinks of all the girls who do get to grow into adulthood as inextricably connected to the girls who are killed. Then Ruth sees an image of a girl who strayed to the bushes and disappeared. Ruth writes the image in her journal. Ruth also listens to the happy screams of the kids at the zoo, which drowns out the sounds of the other kind of screams.

That year Buckley is in seventh grade. He is not athletic like Lindsey, and his favorite teacher is the librarian. Buckley asks his father if he can reclaim his mother's garden. Buckley plants all of his flowers, vegetables and herbs together because he does not see the point of keeping the different kinds of plants separate. Lynn is waiting for the time when Buckley will realize the plants cannot grow together. Buckley hauls some clothes up from the basement to make stakes for his tomato plants. Jack watches Buckley and realizes he is using Susie's clothes. He goes out to take them away from Buckley, and Buckley asks why he can't use them. He is angry—he tells his father he has to choose, and that he is tired of it. Buckley accuses his father of taking the monopoly shoe from his dresser, the one he saved because it was Susie's piece. He tells his father that he acts like Susie was only his, and asks him to think about him and Lindsey. Jack hears a voice that says, "Let go." Suddenly Jack does not feel well, and he has the signs of a heart attack. While Buckley gets Grandma Lynn Jack quietly says that he could never choose because he loved all three of his children.

Susie watches her father in the hospital. She has two conflicting wishes—for him to die so she can be with him forever, and for him not to die. At home Buckley is in bed and he feels very guilty. Lindsey had questioned him about what they were talking about and why their father was so upset. Buckley misses his father tucking him in. Jack would take the top sheet, bunch it up, and then snap it open like a parachute and let it float delicately down onto Buckley. That night Buckley lies in his room without his usual good night from his father, and he begs Susie not to let their father die.

Susie leaves her brother and walks away from the gazebo. The landscape changes and she knows something will be revealed. She sees her grandfather approaching. She remembers dancing with him while standing on his feet when she was six, and she does the same now. They dance to a song that always made her grandfather cry. Once Susie had asked him why; he told her that sometimes people still cry for someone they lost along time ago. As they dance Susie knows something on earth was changing. When the music stops her grandfather leaves. She asks where he is going and he tells her not to worry because she is so close.

Chapter 19

In California, Abigail comes to work at the winery to find a note that says that her mother had called and it is an emergency. She calls the house and there is no answer. She calls the Singhs ad Ruana tells her an ambulance came to the house a few hours ago. Then she calls the local hospitals, and finds the one that Jack is at an they tell her he had a heart attack. She tells her manager and soon she is on a plane on her way to Philadelphia with a transfer in Chicago. In Chicago Abigail calls her mother, Lynn. Lynn tells her he is asking for her, and also gives her the news that Samuel proposed to Lindsey. Then she tells her Jack is asking for Susie as well.

Outside of the Chicago airport, Abigail smokes a cigarette. She is wearing her Krusoe Winery sweatshirt, and her skin is darker, bringing out the blue in her eyes. She wears her hair in a loose ponytail and some of it has begun to gray. She sees that she is in an hourglass—the time she had alone is limited by her attachments that are now pulling her back. She sits down by a pot that contains weeds and a small tree and pulls out her wallet. She pulls out a facedown photo of Susie and looks at it. She misses Susie's teeth, which she had liked to watch grow. In the picture Susie is nervous and has a closed lip grin. She leaves the photo propped up by the little tree and she goes to catch her flight.

On the flight Abigail sits alone between two other seats, She thinks about how if she were traveling as a mother she would have one of her children on either side. She sees that in some ways she has ceased being a mother because she missed so many years of her children's lives. She feels she has been punished because she never wanted to be a mother.

When she arrives at the airport she barely recognizes Lindsey, who is lean and angular. She almost does not see Buckley, a chubby boy sitting off to the side. When she sees him she is reminded of her chubby days when she was twelve, days she was grateful that her daughters did not have to relive. She asks Lindsey how her father is, and Samuel replies that he is not in good shape. Abigail greets Buckley, and he tells her he goes by Buck. Lindsey notices her mother no longer wears rings. They go to the luggage pick up, but Abigail has no luggage. Abigail admits to Lindsey, simply, that she lied to her. A look passes between them, and Susie thinks she sees the secret of Len. They head to the hospital. Lindsey tells her mother that they will not let Buckley visit because of his age. She promises to do something about it, and Buckley says, "Fuck you." She asks him to look at her, and he gives her a look of fury. Abigail cries in the front seat. Samuel says things will be better when they see Mr. Salmon, and turns on the radio.

The hospital is the same one she was at eight years ago when Jack had the incident in the cornfield. Abigail remembers how she felt that night with Len. She wants to go back to California and be among strangers. Then she sees her mother's feet in oxford pumps, and it brings her back. When she walks into Jack's room all of the other people fall away for her. She holds his hand and cries. He greets her as Ocean Eyes, and jokes that this is what it takes to get her to come back. She asks if it is worth it and he says they'll see. He tries to touch her cheek but his arm is weak so she lays her cheek in his palm. Lynn quietly leaves the room. She gets a note that says Len Fenerman is going to visit; she sticks the note in her purse.

Chapter 20

Mr. Harvey goes to Connecticut and finds a tin-roofed shack where he once strangled and buried a waitress. Inside, the grave has been dug up. He falls asleep beside the empty grave.

Susie began to keep a list of the living to counter the list of the dead. She notices the Len Fenerman does the same. They also take note of the living that have been beaten and harmed. Len has only added a few things to Susie's file during the past years: the clue about Sophie Cichetti, the coke bottle, the Pennsylvania keystone charm. He wants to give the charm to Jack Salmon even though that is against the rules. When he sees that Jack is in the hospital he decides he will go and give him the charm. Susie feels both pity and respect for Len because he tries to understand things that are impossible to understand by looking at the physical, just as Susie does.

Outside of the hospital Abigail buys the whole stock of daffodils from a girl selling them and decorates Jack's room with them while he sleeps. The rest of the family has gone home but she is not ready to go there yet. She goes out to get something to eat. She walks through the parking lot where she tries to figure out who the people in the hospital are by looking in the cars; this makes her feel less alone. She goes to a diner and orders food. A man looks at her and she takes in his details; she realizes that while in Pennsylvania she looks at any man like he could be Susie's killer, but she does not do this out West. After she eats she goes back to the hospital. She sits in the lobby and decides she will go up and say good-bye to Jack after spending a few hours with him. She feels relief at this decision.

Abigail goes to Jack's room. Susie is watching and cannot peel herself away. She takes Jack's hand. Susie thinks of the grave rubbing with the dead knight, and how Lindsey used to pretend to be the wife who wants to move on because the knight is stuck in time. Abigail holds Jack's hand for a long time. She leans her head on the pillow next to his. She remembers how that winter she told a young woman that there is always a stronger one and a weaker one in the relationship, but that doesn't mean the weaker one doesn't love the stronger one. She realizes now that she is the weaker one and she wonders how she thought the opposite all those years. Abigail watches Jack and begins to think of the house, and of how she fell in love with him and had Susie. She decides she likes Jack's graying hair. She falls asleep. As they sleep, Susie sings the song that her father used to sing to her and Lindsey, but now she sings it to them, telling them how much she misses them.

At 2 AM it is raining on the tin shack that Mr. Harvey is sleeping in. He is dreaming of the back of Lindsey's soccer shirt as she ran away from his house; he has this dream when he feels threatened, and he marks that moment as the moment his life began to spiral downwards.

At 4 AM Jack's eyes open and he sees that Abigail is asleep next to him on the pillow. He wants to tell her how he felt when Susie died but does not want to wake her. He finds he often has to command himself to think of his two living children. Jack listens to the rain, and he also hears birds; he thinks they must be baby birds that woke up without their mother and he feels the desire to rescue them. Then, Susie slips into the room in a way she has never been able to before, she feels she is present somehow. Susie realizes that her father never stopped being devoted to her as the girl with her whole life ahead of her. Jack senses her and speaks to her. Abigail wakes up and asks Jack how he does it—he tells her there's no choice, and Abigail notes that she chose to run away. He asks if it worked. Susie fades away. Jack notices the room is decorated with daffodils, Susie's flower. He tells her that that is how she does "it"—by living in the face of it.

Abigail tells Jack that seeing their other children was hard. He tells her he fell in love with her again while she was gone. Susie wishes she could be where her mother is because Jack loves her as she grows, instead of how he loves Susie as something that never changes. Jack asks Abigail to stay and she says she will for a while. He tells her Susie was in the room. She acts like she does not believe but he knows she does; she admits to seeing her everywhere in all of the places she goes. She agrees that Jack probably did see her in the room a little while ago. He touches her lips and she parts them. She has to lean down to kiss him. They both cry.

Analysis

Susie is surviving her grief of dying and being stuck in time by watching Lindsey grow up and living vicariously through her. When Lindsey and Samuel decide to get married and repair the house they found, it is symbolic of them building a new life in the wake of Susie's death. Susie notes her sister is neither running away from or towards her—she is just surviving without her and healing. Lindsey now feels even more responsibility for their father's wellbeing.

Buckley also spends much of his time trying to protect his fragile father, but at one point he gets tired of protecting him. Buckley's attempt to use Susie's clothes to stake his tomato plants results in an argument that leads to his father's heart attack. Buckley argues with Jack about how Jack believes Susie is only his, and accuses him of taking the monopoly shoe, referring back to the shoe that Buckley kept when Jack explained Susie's death. For Buckley, the shoe represents Susie, and he feels that Jack wants to keep Susie all for himself so taking the shoe symbolizes him taking

Buckley's right to grieve Susie in his own way. Buckley's decision to stop protecting his father parallels the time when Jack and Lindsey realized they could no longer protect Buckley from Susie's death and they decided to bring him to the impromptu memorial. But in this case, Jack is so fragile that it breaks his heart, almost literally, and he ends up in the hospital. Jack also knows he needs to move on and he hears a voice telling him to let go repeatedly. His surviving the heart attack is symbolic of his surviving the grief of letting go of Susie and finding a way to move on.

The power of the photograph is again brought into play in these chapters, as both Abigail and Jack look at pictures. Jack finds pictures of Abigail that Susie took and he can see the mask she wears. He looks at the photographs when he sees something that makes his heart ache—thus the photographs have a sort of healing effect for him. He also falls in love with Abigail again while he looks at the pictures, demonstrating how powerful a photo can be for the viewer depending on how he interprets the picture.

Abigail also examines a photograph of Susie while she is flying back to see her husband. When she takes out Susie's photograph, it is paralleled with the photo that Len has in the evidence box and Ray keeps in the volume of Indian poetry. Each person's view of that photograph has evolved over time. In a sense, Susie is buried in the photograph; there is no physical gravesite, so all they have is the memories of her that are focused on the image in the picture. She leaves Susie's photograph behind as a symbol of her transition out of the state of trauma and grief, paralleling Jack's heart attack as a way of him transitioning out of that state.

The reason Abigail left was because she did not want the responsibility of grieving Susie, of continuing to be a mother and a wife; when she goes to the hospital, she again feels she wants to be rid of these responsibilities. For Abigail, responsibility is a burden rather than a calling. She feels guilty for this in some ways, especially when her children greet her at the airport and the mood is tense and hostile. Her children are angry with her for leaving them and for leaving their fragile father. Using simile, she compares herself to an hourglass that tells time —the time she had alone is limited by her attachments that are now pulling her back. This alludes again to Persephone, who spends part of her time in the world of the gods and part of her time in the underworld. While Susie watches her mother take her sleeping father's hand, she thinks again of the grave rubbing mentioned in Chapter 7. Susie and Lindsey would role-play as parts of the grave rubbing; Susie is the dead knight and Lindsey is the widow. Lindsey's favorite line was "How can I be expected to be trapped for the rest of my life by a man frozen in time?" (276); here, Abigail feels that if Jack is not able to move on and recover from Susie's murder, that she too will be trapped in that grief.

Absence continues as a theme in these chapters. Mr. Harvey sleeps beside an empty grave; not only is the girl that he killed dead, her body is also gone. Absence is countered by keeping a list of the living—something that Susie, Len and Ruth do. The counterparts to the absent and the lost are those who are still present. Susie has also found a way to be more present on Earth, and she is able to appear for her father in his hospital room. At the same time, Susie is moving towards a new place in heaven—she sees her grandfather, foreshadowing that she will soon be in a different part of heaven with him. On Earth Jack and Abigail finally begin to talk about Susie openly and how each of them deals with it—they are learning how to survive their grief, and fill her absence with their memories. They are building something new together.

Summary and Analysis of Chapter 21-23 & Bones

Chapter 21

Susie leaves her parents to go watch Ray Singh. She remembers how badly she wanted him to kiss her, and how scared she was as well. She had her parents tell her the story of their first kiss. She also asked her Grandma Lynn about it. She tells Susie that her first kiss came from a grown man who was the father of one of her friends. She liked it because he really knew how to kiss. Lynn asks Susie if there is a boy she wants to kiss and she tells her about Ray and how she is scared she won't be good at kissing. Lynn tells her to have fun. When Ray does kiss her by her locker it is such a surprise that she wishes more than anything that she could kiss him again.

Ruth's father cuts an article out from the paper that shows how the developers are going to fill in the sinkhole. Ruth gets into the car with Ray and immediately starts discussing the article with him without saying hello. The article describes filling the "throat" of the hole. They laugh at the detailed description of how they will fill it with cement and dirt. Ray pulls over near new construction. They both spot Joe Ellis, who they know is still living at home. Ruth comments that he never got over it. Susie feels bad for him because Joe was never able to get over the neighborhood's accusations that he killed their pets, and he was also never able to take solace in the love of animals. Animals shied away from him because he is broken.

Len leaves his apartment above a barbershop and heads to the hospital. He has a backpack full of evidence from the murder cases including pictures of recovered gravesites. He realizes that the Salmons will be expecting bigger news, such as the recovery of Susie's body or the arrest of George Harvey, but all he has is the charm. He goes into the hospital and knocks on Jack's door. Len immediately opens with the fact that they have not caught the killer. Jack is visibly disappointed. He says he brought an item of Susie's. Abigail is reminded of the similar way Len had presented the jingle bell hat. He gives them the keystone charm. Jack remembers the charm very clearly. Abigail opens the ziplock and Jack takes the charm out carefully. Len tells them they found the charm next to another girl's grave and that George Harvey is linked to other murders. Jack wants the case to be reopened but Abigail does not. She asks Len to leave. Len knows the sex she had with him was an act of willful forgetting.

While Susie is headed to watch Ray and Ruth she sees George Harvey driving in an orange car that is made of many different parts. His memories of the women he had harmed are slowly coming back to him. He remembers the first woman he raped, a high school acquaintance. He was never tracked down for the crime. The girl died a few years later when her brother fell asleep with a lit cigarette. Now, she sits in the car next to George Harvey. Susie wonders when he will remember her.

Ruth and Ray arrive at the sinkhole. It looks pretty much the same as it did when Susie was put into it, but it has expanded and the Flanagans' house is sinking in. Ruth and Ray walk up to the sinkhole. Susie remembers when she went with her father and Buckley to sink the refrigerator. She remembers walking up to the edge of the hole and feeling it give slightly, like the way mole holes give in a graveyard. She is glad she is mole-proof by being in the safe in the sinkhole. Now, Ruth stands at the edge and Ray tells her that is close enough. They see the earth burp and the corner of a stove rises. Ruth wonders out loud where Susie's body ended up. Susie wants to tell her that she guessed it right. Ray goes to look at the house. Ruth stays by the hole and she sees Susie standing in the place where Mr. Harvey dumped her. Ruth asks her if she wants anything, but Susie vanishes.

That day Hal brings Buckley and Samuel to a bike show, and his bike shop is closed. Buckley's birthday is soon and Hal and Samuel pitched in to buy him a drum kit, as per Lynn's suggestion. Grandma Lynn is at the mall trying to find clothes for Abigail to wear. At the hospital Abigail is reading the newspaper to Jack and he is watching her lips wishing he could kiss her. Lindsey is home alone. Mr. Harvey drives into their neighborhood in the middle of the day. No one notices him except for the mother who now lives in his old house. Harvey watches Lindsey in the window. Susie sees that all of the ghosts of the women and animals Harvey killed are leaving his house and getting into his car with him. The police pull up to him and he tells them he used to live in the neighborhood. The policeman tells him to move on.

Ruth does not tell Ray she saw Susie. She decides she will write it in her journal first. As they head back to the car Ray sees a wild flower that he knows his mother will like to press. As he goes to get it, Ruth sees George Harvey's car coming down the road filled with women in bloody gowns. Then she blacks out, and this is when Susie falls to Earth.

Chapter 22

Ruth collapses onto the road. At the same time, Susie tips out of the gazebo. Ray rushes up to Ruth. For a moment, Susie and Ruth are the same body and then Ruth leaves her body, but not as a dead soul. Susie hears Holiday barking for her and Franny calling to her. Suddenly, they are gone. Susie is in Ruth's body. She opens her eyes to see Ray's gray eyes looking back at her. Ray asks her if she fainted. As Susie gets used to being in Ruth's body, she is able to say she is OK and stand up. She feels she has been given the gift of being back on earth a little longer. Ray tells Ruth that she seems like she changed. Susie asks Ray to kiss her and he does. They walk back to the car hand in hand. In the car he kisses her again; Susie savors the feeling of his stubble. She is very happy because this is what she wanted for so long; in heaven, her friend Holly is happy for her as well.

Ray asks where she wants to go. Susie knows she does not want to chase after Mr. Harvey. She tells him she wants to go to Hal Heckler's bike shop. Ray asks her if he can kiss her again, and she agrees, blushing. While they kiss she sees Ruth in heaven lecturing a group of men in black berets. Susie tells Ray that when they kiss she sees heaven. He asks her to tell him about it. She says that if he makes love to her, she will. They drive toward the bike shop. Ray tells her that when he finishes school he won't move back home; Susie realizes that had she lived she could have had the option to live in other places.

At the bike shop, Susie knows where the key is hidden on top of the door and lets them both in. There is a bedroom and a bathroom there. Susie showers and asks him to come in. He calls her Susie then. She seizes up and tells him what he did. Ray gets in and does not touch her at first. Then he traces a scar on her side—Susie tells him, in third person, that the scar is from Ruth's volleyball incident. Ray realizes that she is not Ruth. Susie tells him she has watched them both. They kiss and Susie cries. She touches him and holds him; she notes the gentleness of this interaction compared to how Mr. Harvey touched her. Susie asks him if he remembers the note he wrote her where he called himself the Moor. He lifts her up, she wraps her legs around him, and then he is inside her. Ray asks her what heaven is like. She tells him it is like anywhere you want to be. Ray knows she will be gone soon. They make love in the shower and in the bedroom. He does not want her to leave, but she knows her time on earth is up. She sees a cloudy mass at the end of the bed. When Ray touches her she can no longer feel him. Susie asks Ray if he ever thinks about the dead, and tells him they are all around him. Ray gets up to go shower. The room fills with spirits. Susie wants to tell him she'll miss him, or thank him, but instead she tells him to read Ruth's journals. Susie calls her house and Buckley picks up but he cannot hear her. Susie realizes she is standing with the rest of the spirits in the room and Ruth is sprawled on the desk. Ray gets out of the shower and rushes to her. She wakes up sleepily. He knows Susie is gone.

When leaving, Susie feels like she is riding backwards on a train through a tunnel, as she did once with her family. The trip back is easier than the trip there was. She watches Ray and Ruth hold each other without speaking about what has happened.

Chapter 23

In the morning, the smell of Ruana's cooking goes up the stairs to where Ruth and Ray lay together. The night before, they had cleaned up Hal's place and then driven home in silence. Ruana found them sleeping together later that night and was grateful that Ray had at least one friend. Ray wakes up around 1 AM and looks at Ruth sleeping and wants to touch her. But then the moon lights up her bag, and he goes and reads her journal. He reads about each murdered woman that Ruth has recorded. She wakes up and sees him and says that she has so much to tell him.

At the hospital, Nurse Eliot helps the Salmons as they leave with Jack in a wheelchair. Buckley steers the wheelchair while Lindsey and Abigail follow behind carrying daffodils. In the elevator Lindsey remembers the daffodils that were lying in the field during the first memorial, and no one knew who put them there. As they enter the lobby, Susie watches all four of them together and knows they are meant to be there, together and alone.

At the Singhs' Ruana pairs apples to make pie to drop off at the Salmons'. After seeing her son curled up with Ruth, she realizes she can't remember when she had last gone to bed at the same time as her husband. She thinks about divorce. When she hears the water running upstairs she calls to them to come down. When they do, she tells Ray that it's late and she wants him to accompany her to the Salmons where she plans to quietly leave the pie on the doorstep. Ruth and Ray are a little overwhelmed, so Ruana slows down. She offers some of the second pie she baked. She asks that they both accompany her to the Salmons'. Ruth says she'll come by later, but she has somewhere she has to be.

Hal and Samuel bring the drum set to the Salmons' as an early birthday present for Buckley because Grandma Lynn knows he'll need it. Lynn offers the two of them drinks, but both of them refuse so she gets water instead. Susie watches her get the water, and realizes she loves Grandma Lynn now more than she ever did on earth. Lynn looks out the kitchen window and sees a girl sitting by Buckley's fort looking at her. The next moment the girl is gone. Lynn decides not to tell anyone.

Susie watches as her father's car pulls into the driveway with her four family members. She wonders if she has been waiting for them to come home together, not to her, but to each other. Buckley helps his father into the house, perhaps protecting him from Abigail. Abigail looks at Lindsey and tells her she looks just like her father's mother. Lindsey and Abigail go to unload the trunk. Lindsey asks her mother if she is going to hurt her father again. Abigail says she will try not to but she is not making promises this time. Lindsey warns Abigail that she knows what she has done (in reference to Abigail sleeping with Len).

Buckley comes outside, very excited about his new drum set. When Abigail gets inside she hands the daffodils to Lynn and goes upstairs to Susie's old room. She stands in the doorway and tells Susie she loves her. Susie realizes she has been waiting to hear this from her mother. She had needed time to know that her love for Susie would not destroy her. Abigail sees a framed picture by the bed: it is the photograph that Susie took of her. Abigail goes to the bathroom where she sees the cream colored towels her mother must have bought. At first she is critical of her choice, but then she realizes she needs to accept her mother as she is. Susie does not appear for her mother in the bathroom; she knows that she is in some way done yearning for her family, although she cannot explain why. She also knows she will always yearn for them and they for her.

Downstairs Hal teaches Buckley how to use the brush on the snare drum. Abigail comes back downstairs and Lynn tells everyone that Samuel has an announcement to make. Lynn brings out champagne. Samuel tells the family that he is happy Mrs. Salmon is home, and that Mr. Salmon is back from the hospital and that he is proud to be marrying their daughter. He bravely kisses Lindsey in front of everyone. Susie sees that the connections between people that had grown in her absence make up the lovely bones of a body. She can now see how things can be without her in the world.

The family goes into the dining room to eat. As they are eating, Hal sees Ray Singh outside. They catch him as he is going back to the car where Ruana is waiting with the motor on. Abigail goes out to invite Ruana and Ray in. Ruana asks Abigail if she will smoke her foreign cigarettes with her again in the future, and Abigail agrees. Inside, Jack invites Ray to sit. He has a special place in his heart for the boy who loved his daughter. Susie realizes that her family and friends will not know she is gone, just like they don't know when she hovers in one room. She sees Ruth walking alone in the cornfield; she knows that she will always be haunted, and that Ruth now has the story of Susie's life and death to tell if she wants to.

While Ruana and Ray are still there, Samuel starts to talk about the house he and Lindsey found off Route 30. Ray asks him more about it, and tells him that Ruth's father owns that house. Mr. Connors bought some old houses in the area and plans on restoring them. Susie leaves.

Bones

No one notices when the dead are leaving, except for those closest to the doors, like Grandma Lynn. She died a few years later, but Susie has not seen her in her heaven yet. She knows she will in time. Susie admits she still sneaks away to watch her family sometimes, just like her family still thinks of her sometimes.

After Lindsey and Samuel get married, they stay at the empty house on Route 30. Mr. Connors agrees to sell it to them—he asks for pay in Samuel's labor for Mr. Connors' new restoration business. Samuel agrees, and they clear the lot and set up a trailer. Lindsey continues to study and Samuel looks for the right doorknobs and other items to fit the house. Lindsey is surprised when she finds out she is pregnant. Jack hopes he will be able to teach another child the love for model-ship building like he did with Susie.

Susie says that heaven is not about safety. They have fun doing things like making Buckley's garden grow with all the plants surviving together. Abigail marvels at this, just as she marvels at most things she notices when she gets back. Susie's parents give all of her possessions and Grandma Lynn's things to Goodwill. They now tell each other whenever they think about Susie. Ray becomes Dr. Singh, and Ruana calls him the real doctor in the family. He still believes that the dead are all around, and that he did make love to Susie. When he is in doubt he calls Ruth. Ruth now lives in a studio apartment on the Lower East Side in New York. She is still trying to find ways to communicate to others that the dead are everywhere and that they talk to people.

Susie is now in what she calls wide wide Heaven because it has all of her desires, from most simple to most grand. Her grandfather calls it comfort. She can now go places that she never imagined in her small heaven dreams.

Susie scans the earth with her grandfather. One day, she sees Mr. Harvey coming out of a bus and going into a diner. She watches as he sees a teenage girl from the bus and follows her out to where she is smoking. He makes a plan in his head of where he can put the body in a near-by ravine. The girl realizes he is creepy and walks away. Susie sees the icicles behind him. After the girl walks away an icicle falls, throws Mr. Harvey off balance, and he pitches into the ravine. His body is not found for weeks because of the snow.

Susie watches Lindsey as she grows a garden. Lindsey thinks about the clients she helps in her job as a therapist. Sometimes it takes her the longest to figure out the simple things; she remembers how it took her a while to figure out that Susie would offer to trim the grass by the fence so she could play with Holiday. Lindsey thinks about how she will need to get her daughter a dog in a few years. Samuel brings their daughter, Abigail Suzanne, out to a blanket near the flowers. Lindsey leaves Susie to her memories.

Five miles away, a man shows his wife a mud-encrusted charm bracelet found in the old industrial lot. They are bulldozing the lot because they are afraid of sinkholes, like the one that swallowed up cars nearby. His wife comments that the little girl must be grown up by now. Susie says, almost, but not quite. She wishes her readers a long and happy life.

Analysis

These chapters lead up to the climax of Susie fulfilling her last earthly wish before she leaves her family and moves on. All of the characters are brought into play in this build up, and after she fulfills her wish, all of the loose ends of the story are tied up.

When Ruth and Ray go to the sinkhole, they are unknowingly going to Susie's grave. The closing up of the sinkhole is symbolic of Susie's finishing her time watching the people she knows on Earth. The sinkhole is personified in the newspaper article—it has a throat, and later it "swallows" cars. Ruth is fascinated with it as a greater power. Again, Susie brings in the image of the safe that her body rests in—she actually does feel safe in there, because she knows her body is protected from moles.

Len also tries to close up the case of Susie's murder by delivering the keystone charm to Jack. Len's guilt "thickens" as he goes into the hospital—he feels guilty for what happened with Abigail. The keystone, which has continuously appeared, and is one of the only items Harvey keeps from Susie and it represents Susie's body, just as her picture does for Abigail.

Although Mr. Harvey is never formally punished for his crimes, he does begin to feel the weight of them. As he drives through the Salmons' neighborhood Mr. Harvey is flooded by the memories of the women he has killed. Prior to this he was able to keep their memories at bay but now they live in his memory too, just as Susie lives in the memories of her loved ones.

When Mr. Harvey is pulled over by the police, he comments that they are building something in the old cornfield—construction where destruction happened, symbolic of building anew. Since Susie's death there has been a lot of building and development in the area—but in the end of the book, they also tear some of it down because the earth swallowed the cars. Again we are reminded that construction and destruction are counterparts that act to balance each other.

By having sex with Ray via Ruth's body, Susie is completing the last act on earth that she has grown to desire in her time in heaven and in watching her peers and family grow up. She also wants to grow up—she wants to be able to leave her loved ones on earth to their lives. Again, the act of sex, like Lindsey's first, is overshadowed by Susie's rape. She seems to feel that in order to ease her pain at the violence of that experience, she needs to have a gentle, loving sexual experience to counter it. Susie savors all the sounds and feelings of being human—the weight of Ruth's body, the smack of Ray's kiss. Knowing that she could have left her hometown to be in another place surprises Susie—yet, her journey in heaven parallels this. She leaves her small heaven for the "wide wide heaven." With the loss of her virginity came the loss of her body as well—now she gains a positive experience with her sexuality and the pleasures of the body.

When Susie sees her family come home together she feels as though she's been waiting for it; she realizes she wants them to heal together as a whole. Hearing her mother say she loves her provides closure for Susie. Susie knows it is time for her to leave her loved ones to their lives, partially because they have come around to a place of accepting her death. Ruth now knows that she owns Susie's story if she chooses to tell it—a comfort to Susie. In the last description of the photograph of Abigail, Abigail is the one viewing the photo. Now, it is no longer the mysterious Abigail, the mother stranger, but simply "a woman staring out across her misty suburban lawn." The picture has evolved from being a mother-stranger to simply being a woman; the photograph has lost some of its power now that Abigail has come to accept both the mother part of her and the "mysterious" part of her. In the end, Susie also comes to accept that she will never really grow up, but she feels she has grown in the course of telling her story and getting through her grief. She too has to accept her absence from the world.

Suggested Essay Questions

1. **Discuss the role that photographs play in the novel.**

   There are two key photographs in the novel: Susie's school picture, and the photograph that Susie took of Abigail. Both the subject of the photograph and the viewer are relevant to this discussion because the view of the photograph can change depending on the subject's maturation, even if the photograph itself remains the same. As the novel progresses, the people who view these photographs see the images differently. Their changing view of the photographs reflects their recovery from the loss of Susie as well as their growth as characters.

2. **Each character feels responsibility and/or guilt in the wake of Susie's death. Choose two or three characters. How do these feelings evolve for these characters throughout the novel?**

   Often the theme of guilt and responsibility is connected to the theme of surviving grief. As each character recovers from his/her grief, their idea of personal responsibility evolves. Any character can be examined here, even Mr. Harvey—although he does not have grief over Susie's death, he does feel a certain responsibility that grows greater as the novel continues.

3. **How is Susie's family able to survive their grief?**

   When Susie's family first hears of her death, they each grieve in their own way and they do not grieve together. As a family, they become isolated from the neighborhood and the town. The theme of construction and destruction is closely related to surviving grief; first the family falls apart (destruction), but they are also able to build new relationships (construction) that help them to move on.

4. **Why is the Inbetween a key component of the action in the novel? What role does it play?**

   The Inbetween is Susie's only method of communicating with the people on earth. It is also the "thick blue line" that Buckley drew to separate heaven and Earth. The separation is important because the novel depicts two different worlds: Susie's heaven, and life on Earth. Thus the Inbetween both connects and separates these worlds.

5. **How could *The Lovely Bones* be framed as a coming of age story?**

   Although Susie dies at age fourteen, she is able to watch her peers as they grow up. She never gets a chance to grow up but she does change and mature in many ways. Her experience with Ray via Ruth's body could be seen as her passage into maturity. Once she has this experience she is able to let go of watching the living world.

6. **Both physical and psychological absence are important to the novel's**

plot. Discuss how absence works as a theme in the novel.

Susie's missing body is the first major absence in the novel. With the absence of her body came the feelings of loss experienced by her family and friends, and they dealt with this absence in different ways. Some of the characters, such as Buckley and Mr. Harvey, use an object to represent someone that is gone; others use a photograph as a way of reminding themselves of a person who is absent. Later in the novel, Abigail also distances herself from her family and leaves them. Both Susie's death and Abigail's absence cause the characters to form the relationships that Susie later refers to as lovely bones.

7. **Discuss how the theme of construction and destruction works in the novel.**

The physical construction and destruction in the novel act as a metaphor for the emotional loss and rebuilding that happen in the wake of Susie's death and other losses. For example, the development of the neighborhood is representative of the growth that happens after Susie's death. The construction of physical structures, such as Buckley's fort and the house that Lindsey and Samuel repair, are symbolic of the characters' emotional recovery from Susie's death. Construction is also represented through the new relationships that form after Susie's death, such as Ruth and Ray's friendship.

8. **How is memory used to further the plot of the story? How is it used as a tool of characterization?**

Susie can see into the thoughts and the memories of the people she watches on earth. She uses these memories to form fuller pictures of the people she knows; through examining memories of others, Susie is able to better understand both her killer and her mother. Memory is also important to the story because Susie lives in the memories of the people who are alive, and the frequency that they think of her and talk of her is indicative of their recovery from grief. As people think and talk of Susie less, she remains in their memories, and she also is able to accept the fact that she is no longer part of the living world.

9. **Many of the characters in the novel feel isolated, or they purposely isolate themselves. How does isolation function to connect the characters? How does it pull them apart?**

When Susie's family first hears of her death, they isolate from each other, and this pulls them apart, especially Jack and Abigail. At the end of the novel they realize that they both felt the pain of Susie's death, and they no longer have to isolate—they can share their memories of Susie with each other. For Ruth and Ray, their isolation brings them together so they can grieve Susie. Susie is isolated in heaven, making her physically apart from her family. But her vantage point also draws her closer to them, as she is able to see what they do and experience as a result of her death. Thus, isolation works in many ways, and each character's isolation evolves throughout the novel.

10. **Even though Susie is dead, she plays a main role in the story-world of the novel. Discuss how her character evolves, and how she affects people on Earth without being present.**

Susie affects people on earth in two ways: she communicates with them from the Inbetween, or she does nothing except exist in their memories. Susie's death and absence function to bring characters together and form connections that would not exist if not for her death. Also, even though Susie is in heaven she is able to grow to a place where she can leave the living. By being with them she had a reciprocal relationship with them in many ways, from across the Inbetween.

Suggested Essay Questions

Narration from Beyond the Grave

Narration from the point of view of the dead character allows for Susie to know everything about what is happening on Earth. This is a useful plot device because there are never any questions for Susie about what is going on in the world of the living. The difference between Susie's narration and the narration of the usual third person omniscient narrator is that Susie plays a key role in the plot; her murder is the main conflict of the novel, and the way the living characters come to terms with her loss is the primary action of the novel. With a third person omniscient voice, the narrator does not play a role in the lives of the other characters. It is not a person necessarily—it is just a voice that knows all that is going on in the characters' lives. However, Susie is a first person omniscient narrator with her own plot progressing in heaven. She, like her living counterparts, also goes through character growth and development in the course of the novel.

The three traditional formats of a plot with a dead narrator are biography (when told post-mortem this is known as autothanatography), murder mystery or ghost story. Sebold's novel does not conform to any of these—the story is not a biography of Susie's life, it is not a mystery, because she tells us her killer in the first chapter, and it cannot be exclusively classified as a ghost story either—but it may be a combination of the three. *The Lovely Bones* does fit one aspect of the after-death narration, as classified by scholar Alice Bennett: the meaning of the story lies in the end. From the after-death point of view, Susie is able to gather her own evidence about her family and her murder. In essence, she solves the "mystery" of her own life. Bennett asserts, "The conclusion of death writing is non-existence and absence, not fully realized presence" (465-66). This proves to be true for *The Lovely Bones*; at the end of the novel, the answer of how Susie's murder and loss is resolved is presented in the figurative "lovely bones" that Susie sees growing in her absence.

In writing Susie's story from the after-death point-of-view, Sebold suggests the dead and the living have a reciprocal relationship, instead of the traditional idea that the living have a one-way relationship with the dead and have to go through their own grieving process. In an interview with the Guardian, Sebold reported that readers have told her they found this narration from beyond the grave comforting because it helps them imagine their loved ones are safe in heaven, and watching the living.

Author of ClassicNote and Sources

Rachel Younger, author of ClassicNote. Completed on September 12, 2010, copyright held by GradeSaver.

Updated and revised Elizabeth Weinbloom December 30, 2010. Copyright held by GradeSaver.

Sebold, Alice. The Lovely Bones. New York: Little, Brown and Company, 2002.

Viner, Katharine. "Above and Beyond." guardian.co.uk. 2002-08-24. 2010-08-19. <http://www.guardian.co.uk/books/2002/aug/24/fiction.features>.

"Alice Sebold." *Contemporary Authors Online*. Gale Literary Databases, 2010. Web. 20 August, 2010.

Bliss, Ann. Studies, "'Share Moments, Share Life': The Domestic Photograph as a Symbol of Disruption and Trauma in *The Lovely Bones*." *Womens' Studies* 37.7 (2008): 1–30. *ProQuest*. Web. 20 August 2010.

Bennett, Alice. "Unquiet Spirits: Death Writing in Contemporary Fiction." *Textual Practice* 23.3 (2009): 463-479. *ProQuest*. Web. 20 August 2010.

Tidy, Samantha. "Vol. II: Heaven as it is on Earth: Representations of Literary Heavens in Contemporary Literature, with a Focus on Alice Sebold's *The Lovely Bones*." Diss. RMIT University, 2009. *ProQuest Digital Dissertations*. Web. 20 August 2010.

Mandel, Naomi. "The Contours of Loss." *Criticism* 50.4 (2008): 663-673. *Project Muse*. Web. 20 August 2010.

Alber, Jan. "Impossible Storyworlds-- and What to Do with Them." *Storyworlds: A Journal of Narrative Studies* 1 (2009): 79-96. *Project Muse*. Web. 20 August 2010.

Essay: The Lovely Bones by Alice Sebold

by Jessica Tamol
May 29, 2009

The Lovely Bones

By Alice Sebold

This story takes place in suburban Pennsylvania in 1973.

Susie Salmon is the protagonist and narrator of this story. The reader takes a front seat ride in Susie's story of her rape and murder and understands what she is going through as she watches how her family and the people around her cope with her murder. Susie was murdered at the age of fourteen in Philadelphia and was brutally killed by a serial killer in a cornfield near her house. It is later discovered by the police that Susie's neighbor, Mr. Harvey, was the rapist and killer of Susie and many other girls, including Harvey's wife. While Susie watches her family from heaven, she also makes several attempts to help the earthbound find her murderer and comfort those who feel sorrow and pain from her misfortunate passing. Susie was the oldest in her family and had a younger sister and brother. Susie also had a crush in high school named Ray Singh, who was also in love with her. Later discovered by the police was a note from Ray to Susie proclaiming his lover to her, and was evidence making him a suspect in her murder investigation. With a solid alibi, all accusations were dropped.

Jack Salmon is the father of Susie, Lindsey, and Buckley, and the wife of Abigail. After the loss of his daughter Susie, Jack is seen as attached an unable to let go of her death. Susie and Jack had a very close father-daughter relationship and this is seen when Jack has such an unimaginably difficult time coping with his loss. He is seen sometimes in his daughter's old room, remembering her for what a great person she was and missing her terribly. Jack even had to stop some of the hobbies that he loved because the memories of his deceased daughter were too much to bear. For example, jack stopped making boats in bottles because that was a project that he and Susie used to do together. Once when Jack got very sad and upset, he destroyed all of his sailboats and bottles because of the painful memories that they brought back. Jack also had neglected his patriarchal duties to his other children shortly after Susie's death. It was only after Abigail explained to him that his other children are still alive and without a father that he stepped up and became a father that Susie would be proud of. Then, Jack bonded greatly with Buckley but had a difficult time with Lindsey because when he looked at her, he, like many others, would only see the shadow of Susie. But as time passes in the novel, he ends up getting close to Lindsey as well and is basically the father that he used to be before the incident. Jack is also the only character who without a doubt knows that the man who murdered his daughter is Mr. Harvey. He even goes to the extent of assaulting him and trespassing on his property in the hopes of finding evidence to convict him of this crime. This determination to find the killer of his daughter turns out to be a success because in the end of the novel, it is seen that Mr. Harvey is caught and was discovered as being the convict because of the eyes that jack drew towards Harvey.

Abigail Salmon is the mother of Susie, Lindsey, and Buckley and the husband of Jack Salmon. Abigail is the parent who runs the household and takes care of the children while Jack is away at work. After Susie goes missing and is believed to be dead, Abigail is the one person who undoubtedly had faith that her daughter was still alive, even after the majority of the evidence presented itself to say otherwise. After her death was guaranteed, Abigail was a wreck and had her mother fly in to comfort her and help manage the family. After Susie's death, Abigail decided to make a life changing decision and be more than a mother. Therefore, she abandoned her family and went to California to work at a winery. This was her way of coping with the death of her eldest daughter and the fact that her husband was obsessed in finding the murderer of their daughter with no regard of its effect on their remaining two children. Also, while dealing with the drama and sorrow of the murder investigation, Abigail found comfort in the head investigator of the crime, Detective Len Fenerman. While mourning for her daughter, Abigail had a brief affair with this man before she left for her new life in California. Then, when Jack is in the hospital towards the end of the novel and Abigail returns, they have another sexual encounter for old times sake in a private room in the hospital.

This story is about a girl named Susie Salmon and her observing her family from heaven after she was raped and murdered at the age of fourteen by her neighbor. Susie was a smart and very kind girl who was well-liked by her peers. With her death comes a great deal of sorrow from the town in which she lived and also by her family. Each family member coped with her murder in a different way and Susie was watching down from her heaven to observe it all and watch out for those that she cared about most. Jack Salmon, the father, spends most of the story looking for the man who murdered his oldest daughter and finally lets her go by spending a great deal of time with his remaining two children and telling stories about Susie to then a few years after her passing. Abigail, Susie's mother, tends to react in a different way. She becomes unfaithful to her husband with the lead detective o the case of her daughter's investigation and ends up moving out of Pennsylvania altogether and went to live in California and work in a winery. Lindsey and Buckley both manage to live with their sister's murder but grow up looking at life differently than most other children their age because of the experiences that they both went through during this time of mourning. As Susie watches all of this from heaven, she tires to find her inner heaven and her place of peace. She is not able to let go though until her murder is solved and her family is able to move on and let her memory go in order to live their lives in happiness. Susie also tries to help her family and friends find her rapist and murderer and in the end of the novel, ends up killing him with an icicle from heaven and having his body fall into a ravine to be discovered weeks later. After her family finally got into a pattern of living without her comfortably and after Mr. Harvey was found guilty and killed, Susie finally was able to go to a deeper

Essay: The Lovely Bones by Alice Sebold

heaven and live above in a more peaceful place, where she would wait to be reunited with her family once again.

The Lovely Bones by Alice Sebold is a memorable and emotional story about a young girl with a bright future ruined by her being brutally raped and murdered by an unsuspecting neighbor. Throughout Susie's journey in her heaven, her story and adventure gives hope to the readers of this novel and show that there is always a bright side to a story no matter how depressing some parts may be. This inspiration is shown by some of the major ideas of this story, conflicts seen in the family's lives, and a few of the rhetorical strategies used by Alice Sebold in the creation of this novel. One of the major themes in this book is that there is always somebody there to help you when you need it most and that someone is always looking out for you. Another theme of this novel is to believe in your gut instinct. Lastly, another theme seen in this outstanding novel is that the heart heals over time. Some of the conflicts present were man vs. man and man vs. himself. Lastly, some of the rhetorical strategies used to make this novel inspiring to so many were characterization, irony, and language.

The themes in this novel help the reader see that hope is always present. The first major theme that shows this belief is that there is always somebody there to look out for you. This novel basically follows Susie as she is watching out for her family members and friends after her departure with the world. This entire idea effortlessly gives readers the idea that someone is there with them looking over their shoulder and protecting them form the troubles that they face from day to day life. Also, the way that Samuel (Lindsey's best friend, boyfriend, and later husband) is there for Lindsey shows that best friends will always be there for each other when the going gets rough and that true love will conquer even the most depressing memories and events in life. Another theme that supports the thesis effortlessly is the idea that it is necessary to believe in your gut instinct. Throughout the murder investigation, Susie's father Jack had a feeling that Mr. Harvey was not sharing everything that he knew about his daughter's disappearance, and then murder. As Jack kept his eyes open, he discovered a lie that Mr. Harvey had told him and continued to do an investigation of his own. The results of this investigation clearly incriminated Mr. Harvey and it turned out that Jack's first instinct was correct all along and Mr. Harvey was found guilty by the police. As you can see, the fact that Jack believed in himself helps show readers that having hope in yourself results in a positive outcome. Lastly, another present theme proving true the thesis is the idea that the heart heals over time. The entire Salmon family all went thorough one of the most dramatic experiences anybody could ever experience: the loss of a loved one. As the novel progresses, it is seen that with the presence of family and friends, and of course time itself, the heart can manage to heal from even the most terrible wounds, like the death of Susie.

Some of the present conflicts that show the reader that hope is evident in life is man vs. man. The most obvious conflict of man vs. man would have to be the struggle, rape, and murder of fourteen year old Susie Salmon by a neighbor Mr. Harvey. This struggle was physical and took place underground in a hut that Mr. Harvey dug out and lured Susie into. This tragic crime in a way shows hope because of the justice finally given to Susie when Harvey dies at the end of the novel while trying to lure a girl to kill. When the icicle falls, this is the last part of the business that was keeping Susie from crossing over to the deeper heaven. Clearly, even though this struggle took place, hope is still found in the aftermath. Another struggle present is man vs. himself. This struggle is an internal battle that took place inside every character in the novel. This instance is one thing that makes this book different from many others: the internal battle occurring in each character had to do with the protagonist, Susie's murder, specifically her family. Seeing as in the end of the novel, each character came to peace with Susie's death, this struggle shows that hope is all that is needed in order to carry on through rough patches in life.

Also seen in this spectacular novel is the rhetorical strategies and linguistic devices that were brilliantly used by the author of this novel, Alice Sebold. Three of the main devices present that prove the thesis true would have to be characterization, irony, and language. First, the characterization of Susie shows hope on many different ways. The fact that Sebold created Susie to watch over her family in heaven shows readers that they can take comfort in heaven. It could also be interpreted as comforting for them to know that someone is always watching out for them in times of need. A second strategy that is used ingeniously would have to be irony. For example, when Lindsey goes to camp for being smart during the summer and their project is to plan the perfect murder, Lindsey states that death by an icicle would be perfect because the evidence would simply melt away. The irony in this situation is that Susie killed Mr. Harvey from heaven by making an icicle hit him and make him fall down into the ravine. Clearly, this instance shows that hope is evident because everybody who does wrong gets a fitting punishment to their crime in time. Lastly, another device used wisely by the author would have to be the interesting use of metaphors. The novel was written in such a way that the words flowed gently from on paragraph to the next. One of the factors that contributed to this lovely transitional style of writing was a metaphor found on page 309:

"Because horror on Earth is real and it is every day. It is like a

Flower or like the sun; it cannot be contained."

-Alice Sebold

This use of a metaphor creates a visual for the reader and a powerful comparison for them to relate to easily. Even though the quote is talking about horror, it is showing hope because of the description of the way Susie got justice by Harvey's death after the metaphor was stated.

Throughout the novel The Lovely Bones, Alice Sebold used many brilliant techniques that excelled her writing to the next level and also showed that hope is to be evident in the lives of everyone. Some of the ways that hope is shown are through themes, conflicts, and literary elements. Most of the themes were of the necessity of moving on after tragedies and that there is always someone there when a person needs them to be, even if that person can't be seen. The conflicts present were between Harvey and Susie and each one of the members of Susie's family and themselves. These two conflicts showed hope was present by the justice that Susie got and by the inner growth of each character. The amazingly used characterization showed of hope in the way that Susie acted almost as a guardian angel for many of her peers and family. In addition to these great techniques, irony is depicted through Harvey's murder and the relation to the icicle being Lindsey's idea one year in summer camp. In addition, the use of metaphors made the transition from sentence to sentence flow much more smoothly and captured the reader's attention, allowing them to grasp the concept of hope more easily. As you can see, even though this novel may have its fair share of depressing and sad points, it also shows a great deal of strength, love, and hope by just about every character in the novel.

Essay: The Lovely Bones by Alice Sebold

Essay: essay 3

by Anonymous
May 01, 2009

The novel The Lovely Bones by Alice Sebold fits the mold of the Gothic novel genre in several ways that I will talk about in this essay. Even though the novel is very disturbing as well as tragic in several parts, it is still a fantastic story of a girl, who's life was taken way too early, and her family's struggle to cope. The author did an incredible job of turning a disturbing story into an extremely hard-to put-down novel that became a best-seller.

The plot of The Lovely Bones is not a complex one, but has many twists and turns. Susie Salmon is the main character, who while one day on her way home from junior high, takes a short cut through the cornfield bordering her subdivision in rural Pennsylvania. A neighbor named George Harvey talks her into exploring the room he made under the earth in the middle of the cornfield. Susie was very intrigued because she had an interest in science and nature, so she follows him into the room Harvey calls "a little hiding place". Once inside, he raped and stabbed her to death. After this occurred, he dismembers her small body and transfers it into his garage to hide from the police; which after some time he takes it to a sinkhole a couple miles out of town to discard. Her family, which consists of her mother, father, and her younger sister and brother are stunned and start to lose the ability to interact with each other.

Throughout the novel Susie watches her family from her Heaven, which is not just the Heaven everyone goes to, but it is made especially for her. Everything she wished for on Earth is there, and everything she wishes for in Heaven appears before her eyes. Meanwhile, her family tries to move on and deal with the shock of her death. Her father and sister try to investigate and catch the killer, while her mother becomes very detached from the family and eventually has an affair with the police officer that handles Susie's case, eventually leaving her husband. Susie's father eventually suffers a heart attack which brings his wife back to him, and her sister, Lindsay eventually gets married to her high school sweetheart.

Throughout the novel there are many motifs that prove this to be a Gothic novel. First, the horror of Susie's rape, murder, and dismemberment equals if not exceeds the "horror" or "terror" as a prime leitmotif that is used to shock and entertain the reader in Frankenstein by Mary Shelley. In Shelley's sustainment of terror the result of his inability to accept responsibility for the monster he created is clearly shown. The monster terrorizes Victor because he begged and pleaded for him to create a mate or someone for him so he wouldn't be so lonely, which he refused to do. This resulted in the monster brutally killing Victor's loved ones in the hope of scaring Victor into creating him someone to be with. The monster's actions do not have the effects he hopes they will have on Victor. "Horror" as a theme in the novel is shown through the disturbing way that the monster was created in the first place, which is that Victor Frankenstein used dead body parts to create life. This way of creating life is not only horrifying but also grotesque. In both novels terror is a reoccurring theme and definitely entertains the reader as well as disturbs them.

The next example is that Susie goes to a new kind of Heaven after she has been killed. The use of Heaven and Hell is also a general concept that is used in Gothic novels. When Susie reaches Heaven, it isn't anything like she imagined. It is catered to fit her wants and needs, and the people that are also there are people that have left Earth too early as well, something the reader doesn't realize in the beginning of the novel. The use of Hell, as opposed to Heaven, is used a theme in the novel The Monk by Matthew Gregory Lewis. In The Monk, the main character is a monk named Ambrosio. In the novel he is attracted to a woman named Matilda, who is his pupil, which whom he has an affair with. Matilda later reveals herself to be a representative of the Devil, and uses her sinful powers to aid Ambrosio in the rape and killing of an innocent girl named Antonia. In the end Ambrosio sells his soul to the Devil to escape death but doesn't benefit him since in the end of the novel the Devil delivers the monk's prolonged awful death.

The novel Melmoth the Wanderer by Charles Maturin also uses Hell to outline punishment and terror in a Gothic novel. In this novel, the main character is John Melmoth, and he sells his soul to the Devil in order to live 150 extra years. However, he spends all of that time searching for someone else to take his offer that the Devil made him, and in the end is not successful and is forced to retreat to Hell with the Devil himself.

Comparing The Lovely Bones to this novel, a similarity is the idea of getting what one deserves. In Melmoth the Wanderer, John is presented with something that is obviously wrong and may very well not benefit him in any way, but he chooses it anyway. Therefore, John gets what he deserves in the end by being sent to Hell. On the other hand, in The Lovely Bones, Susie's entire life is taken from her in one of the most humanly awful ways possible. By finally learning to let go of her loved ones on Earth, she gets what she deserves in a way by being transferred to the main Heaven which makes her happy. Obviously in contrasting the two novels, the fact that one focuses on Heaven while the other focuses on Hell is one that is significant in the way that it is possible to conduct a Gothic novel around either Heaven or Hell, not just one. Both of these Gothic novels share the use of Heaven and Hell, and are not by far the only two that use Heaven and Hell as supernatural themes to be considered a Gothic novel. These two novels further prove my point that The Lovely Bones is considered a Gothic novel, even though it has a modern twist.

The next way that The Lovely Bones echoes the Gothic genre is when Susie leaves her body to go to her Heaven, a significant event happens. Her soul brushes a classmate of hers, Ruth, and Ruth feels it and knows that something supernatural has happened. Ruth is haunted by this incident for the remainder of the novel and as a result of this event she devotes her life to writing about the visions of the dead she sees. A Gothic novel that this compares to is The Castle of Otranto by Horace Walpole. In this Gothic novel, the plot is that the main character, Manfred, wants his legacy to continue after his son is killed. His wife cannot produce children for medical reasons, so he tries to seduce his son's fiancé that was left behind after his death. During a scene in the novel, the fiancé, Isabella, is hiding from Manfred and is visited by what is thought to be her dead fiance's ghost. Manfred is also visited by supernatural events that obviously scare him and force him to think about the actions he is taking to continue his line of sons.

Following the previous point, the next point that echoes The Lovely Bones is about Susie's father, Jack, who is the one person that has almost devoted his life to finding Susie's killer. In the novel, when he first starts searching for clues and investigating Mr. Harvey by himself, Susie shows her face to him. He is in his study and had just finished smashing all of his bottles of ships out of frustration with Susie's case when she showed her face in the reflection of one of the pieces of glass for a split second. He sees this, and because of this supernatural event he becomes more determined to investigate her case and get revenge on her killer. This event also shows the reoccurring use of supernatural events in this story which classify it as a Gothic novel.

The next event is a very significant one, and also the event that proves this novel to be considered in the Gothic genre. It is toward the end of the novel, when Ruth and Susie's middle school crush, Ray, are at the site of the sinkhole where Susie's body lays. Overcome with emotion for Ray, Susie's soul switches with Ruth's in her body and Susie is enabled to finally get what she always wanted, which was to make love to Ray. They switch places and after it was over Susie returns to Heaven. This event is one that, to me, shows that this book has all the qualities of a Gothic novel. It is a significant supernatural event that not only gives closure to Susie with her Love, but also to the reader in a sense. This event also connects to the Gothic novel Dr. Jekyll and Mr. Hyde by Robert Louis Stevenson, in which Dr. Jekyll is a doctor who, in experimenting with potions, discovers a way to release his most inner feelings of anger and rage in another form of himself. He creates Mr. Hyde, his other side, who he can use to kill and commit horrifying crimes that his conscious can't control. These two novels share the supernatural experience of switching bodies, as well as minds.

My last point that The Lovely Bones is a Gothic novel is when George Harvey, Susie's killer, gets what he deserves. In the end of the novel, after Susie watched the extremely hard journey her family endured after her death and all that they dealt with, she received the satisfaction of watching her killer get what he deserved. After the police uncovered the bodies of all the other girls Harvey killed before Susie, showing he was a serial killer, he was on the run. While he was in a diner trying to escape his past, his lust to kill overtook him and he tried to seduce another young girl. However, the girl denied him. On his way out of the diner, an enormous icicle broke off from the roof and landed on Harvey's head and caused him to fall into a ravine to his death. This event can be compared to many of the Gothic novels we have read also, since a brutal death is a common theme in Gothic novels. For example, in Frankenstein, the monster brutally kills Victor's wife and maid from his home in revenge for not providing him with a mate.

The ending of this novel is significant in the way that it shows irony in the death of the villain of the novel. After he has brutally taken Susie's life, he dumped her body into a sinkhole that ironically Susie's dad had taken her to see when she was younger since it was a strange happening of the Earth that interested her. Also, the ravine Harvey falls to his death in can be compared to the hole in the ground he killed Susie in, and also the sinkhole where Susie's body rested. My point is that the ending of this novel ties together many of the events that occurred throughout the novel, mainly the hole Susie was killed in, the way she was killed, the hole he dumped her in, and finally the ravine Harvey died in. Also, the fact that when Susie was alive, since she had a fascination with nature and Earth in general, the place she died, was buried, and the way George Harvey was killed are all tied together in the significant fact that they are take place in and around something that she loved.

After presenting the Gothic novels The Lovely Bones echoes I have shown in this essay, I believe I have proved the point of The Lovely Bones being considered a Gothic novel. All of the supernatural events, terror, and use of a villain in the novel show the way that this novel fits into the Gothic genre, and also that this novel is an excellent read and very entertaining story that anyone who even remotely likes the Gothic genre will enjoy.

Quiz 1

1. **What animal is inside the snow globe that Susie describes in the epigraph?**
   A. A person
   B. A penguin
   C. A dog
   D. A polar bear

2. **How does Mr. Harvey kill Susie?**
   A. He falls asleep on top of her
   B. He uses a kitchen knife
   C. He strangles her
   D. He uses razor blades

3. **What does Mr. Harvey keep in the dugout that Susie finds particularly strange?**
   A. Shelves
   B. Coca-cola
   C. A book of sonnets
   D. Razor blades and shaving cream

4. **Who is Susie's favorite teacher?**
   A. Mrs. Delminico
   B. Mr. Botte
   C. Principal Caden
   D. Mrs. Dewitt

5. **What is Susie wearing the day she dies?**
   A. A white nightgown
   B. One of Clarissa's dresses
   C. A green skirt and danskin tights
   D. Her yellow elephant bellbottoms

6. **What does Susie say repeatedly while Mr. Harvey rapes her?**
   A. "Please" and "Don't"
   B. "No"
   C. She just screams
   D. "Stop"

7. **What does Mr. Harvey use to gag Susie?**
    A. A hankerchief
    B. Her sock
    C. Her glove
    D. The hat her mother made her

8. **What grade is Susie in when she dies?**
    A. 7th
    B. 8th
    C. 9th
    D. 10th

9. **Who was Susie's best friend in life?**
    A. Clarissa
    B. Ray
    C. Ruth
    D. Holly

10. **Who is Susie's best friend in heaven?**
    A. Franny
    B. Ruth
    C. Holly
    D. Mrs. Utemeyer

11. **Why do the police think Susie is dead?**
    A. There is too much blood in the earth
    B. She has been missing too long
    C. They have her elbow
    D. They found her body

12. **How does Lindsey react when she finds out the police found Susie's elbow?**
    A. She storms to her room
    B. She cries
    C. She vomits
    D. She screams

13. **What book does the police find while they are searching the cornfield?**
    A. To Kill a Mockingbird
    B. Moliere
    C. Othello
    D. Are You There God? It's Me, Margaret

14. **Who identifies the book as a book that is read in Susie's grade?**
    A. Mr. Botte
    B. Mrs. Stead
    C. Ray Singh
    D. Mrs. Dewitt

15. **In heaven, Holly and Mrs. Utemeyer play a duet on which instruments?**
    A. Holly on violin and Mrs. Utemeyer on cello
    B. Mrs. Utemeyer on piano and Holly on guitar
    C. Holly on horn and Mrs. Utemeyer on violin
    D. Mrs. Utemeyer on horn and Holly on violin

16. **Who did Susie's soul "touch" as she was leaving earth?**
    A. Mr. Botte
    B. Lindsey Salmon
    C. Ray Singh
    D. Ruth Connors

17. **What does Ruth steal from Clarissa's locker?**
    A. Nothing
    B. Pictures of Susie and Clarissa's weed
    C. Clarissa's money
    D. Pictures of Susie and Brian's weed

18. **How old was Susie when she took the picture of her mother that is mentioned repeatedly throughout the novel?**
    A. 10
    B. 11
    C. 12
    D. 14

19. **Who is the first person to discover the photograph of Abigail after Susie's death?**
    A. Abigail
    B. Buckley
    C. Lindsey
    D. Jack

20. **When is the first time Susie accidentally "breaks" the Inbetween by appearing?**
    A. When Ruth sees Susie by the sinkhole
    B. When Lynn sees Susie by Buckley's fort
    C. When Buckley sees Susie under the grandfather clock
    D. When her father smashes his model ships

21. **Where does Mr. Harvey put Susie's body?**
    A. He buries it in Connecticut
    B. He buries it in the cornfield
    C. In a safe in the sinkhole
    D. In a refrigerator in the sinkhole

22. **What item of Susie's does Mr. Harvey keep?**
    A. An amber pendant
    B. An eraser shaped like a cartoon
    C. Her charm bracelet
    D. Her Pennsylvania keystone charm

23. **What is Mr. Harvey building in his yard when Jack Salmon offers to help?**
    A. A garden
    B. A cave
    C. A hole
    D. A tent

24. **How does Jack Salmon come to suspect that George Harvey murdered Susie?**
    A. Susie makes a geranium bloom as a sign that Mr. Harvey is guilty
    B. Jack finds concrete evidence that Mr. Harvey did it
    C. He gets a feeling that Mr. Harvey did it
    D. Susie tells her father and he hears her

25. **What is Mr. Harvey's dead wife's name?**

    A. Sophie

    B. Leah

    C. Flora

    D. He was never married

Quiz 1 Answer Key

1. **(B)** A penguin
2. **(B)** He uses a kitchen knife
3. **(D)** Razor blades and shaving cream
4. **(B)** Mr. Botte
5. **(D)** Her yellow elephant bellbottoms
6. **(A)** "Please" and "Don't"
7. **(D)** The hat her mother made her
8. **(C)** 9th
9. **(A)** Clarissa
10. **(C)** Holly
11. **(A)** There is too much blood in the earth
12. **(C)** She vomits
13. **(A)** To Kill a Mockingbird
14. **(B)** Mrs. Stead
15. **(C)** Holly on horn and Mrs. Utemeyer on violin
16. **(D)** Ruth Connors
17. **(D)** Pictures of Susie and Brian's weed
18. **(B)** 11
19. **(C)** Lindsey
20. **(D)** When her father smashes his model ships
21. **(C)** In a safe in the sinkhole
22. **(D)** Her Pennsylvania keystone charm
23. **(D)** A tent
24. **(C)** He gets a feeling that Mr. Harvey did it
25. **(D)** He was never married

Quiz 2

1. **What does Samuel Heckler give Lindsey on Christmas?**
   A. a half-heart necklace
   B. A kiss and a half heart necklace
   C. A song he plays on his saxophone
   D. A kiss

2. **How does Jack Salmon explain Susie's death to his son Buckley?**
   A. Lindsey is the one who explains it
   B. He uses the game of monopoly
   C. He tells Buckley Susie is on an extended sleepover
   D. He never explains it to Buckley

3. **Where does Susie have her first kiss?**
   A. After her death, with Ray when she is in Ruth's body
   B. In the hole in the cornfield, with Mr. Harvey
   C. On the scaffolding in the theater with Ray Singh
   D. By her locker with Ray Singh

4. **What does Ruth get in trouble for at school?**
   A. Skipping class
   B. Drinking alcohol before school
   C. Smoking pot
   D. Drawing a picture of a naked woman

5. **30. How does Len Fenerman's wife die?**
   A. Suicide
   B. She was murdered
   C. An accident
   D. She was sick

6. **Which item caused Abigail the most grief when the police were searching for Susie's body?**
   A. The hat she had made for Susie
   B. Susie's copy of To Kill a Mockingbird
   C. Susie's Pennsylvania keystone charm
   D. Susie's elbow

7. **What does Len Fenerman plan to write on the backs of the photographs he keeps in his wallet?**
    A. The person's name
    B. The date the person died
    C. How the person was killed
    D. The date he solves the case

8. **What do Nate and Buckley look at in Susie's old room?**
    A. Her ghost
    B. The candy she kept under her bed
    C. The photograph of Abigail
    D. The twig she has wrapped in a hankerchief

9. **What was Mr. Harvey's father's profession?**
    A. Driver
    B. Builder
    C. Carpenter
    D. Theif

10. **What is in Grandma Lynn's "bag o' magic"**
    A. Make-up
    B. Alcohol
    C. Her mink
    D. Pills

11. **Who does not come to Lindsey's official memorial service?**
    A. George Harvey
    B. Abigail Salmon
    C. Ray Singh
    D. Ruth Connors

12. **Why does Lindsey faint at the memorial service?**
    A. She sees George Harvey
    B. She doesn't faint
    C. She is very upset
    D. She realizes Susie is dead

13. **Which characters go to the Gifted Symposium?**
    A. Lindsey, Samuel, and Ray
    B. Lindsey, Samuel, and Ruth
    C. Lindsey and Samuel
    D. Lindsey, Ruth and Ray

14. **Where does Lindsey lose her virginity?**
    A. Underneath a boat on the land
    B. In her dorm
    C. In the trees
    D. In a boat on the lake

15. **What does Mr. Harvey do for a living?**
    A. He builds doll houses
    B. He steals
    C. He builds houses
    D. He constructs clubhouses

16. **What does Mr. Harvey's mother give him before she leaves?**
    A. A letter
    B. Her wedding ring
    C. Her amber pendant
    D. A charm from her bracelet

17. **Who beats up Jack Salmon in the cornfield?**
    A. George Harvey
    B. Mr. Botte
    C. Clarissa
    D. Brian Nelson

18. **What kinds of stories would Abigail tell her daughters while she bathed them?**
    A. Stories from picture books
    B. Irish folklore
    C. Fairy tales
    D. Greek myths

19. Why does Abigail want to sleep with Len Fenerman?
A. Because she loves him
B. Because she is not longer in love with Jack
C. Because she wants to forget about her own problems
D. Because he is pursuing her

20. What sport does Lindsey play?
A. Soccer
B. She runs track
C. Softball
D. She runs cross-country

21. What evidence does Lindsey find in Mr. Harvey's house?
A. The knife he used to kill Susie
B. Susie's Pennsylvania keystone charm
C. A drawing he did of the dugout in the cornfield
D. Susie's bones

22. What is the number on the back of Lindsey's sport shirt?
A. 4
B. 5
C. 6
D. 11

23. Who does Susie tell her story to in heaven?
A. Franny
B. Mr. Harvey's other victims
C. Holly
D. Ruth Connors

24. Where does Abigail have sex with Len Fenerman?
A. At the hospital
B. In his car
C. At a hotel
D. In the inner workings of the mall

25. 50. What does Ruth do to mark the anniversary of Susie's death?

A. She writes a poem

B. She leaves daffodils in the cornfield

C. She gets candles and asks Ray to go to the cornfield with her

D. She organizes a memorial service

Quiz 2 Answer Key

1. **(B)** A kiss and a half heart necklace
2. **(B)** He uses the game of monopoly
3. **(D)** By her locker with Ray Singh
4. **(D)** Drawing a picture of a naked woman
5. **(A)** Suicide
6. **(A)** The hat she had made for Susie
7. **(D)** The date he solves the case
8. **(D)** The twig she has wrapped in a hankerchief
9. **(B)** Builder
10. **(A)** Make-up
11. **(C)** Ray Singh
12. **(A)** She sees George Harvey
13. **(B)** Lindsey, Samuel, and Ruth
14. **(A)** Underneath a boat on the land
15. **(A)** He builds doll houses
16. **(C)** Her amber pendant
17. **(D)** Brian Nelson
18. **(D)** Greek myths
19. **(C)** Because she wants to forget about her own problems
20. **(A)** Soccer
21. **(C)** A drawing he did of the dugout in the cornfield
22. **(B)** 5
23. **(B)** Mr. Harvey's other victims
24. **(D)** In the inner workings of the mall
25. **(C)** She gets candles and asks Ray to go to the cornfield with her

Quiz 3

1. **Why does Dr. Singh frequently come home late?**
   A. He is having an affair
   B. He is too absorbed in his work
   C. He has a student who needs help
   D. He works far away from home

2. **Why doesn't Abigail want to go to the cornfield on the one-year anniversary of Susie's death?**
   A. She would rather read
   B. She says she is done with that
   C. She wasn't invited
   D. It makes her too sad

3. **Who left the daffodils in the cornfield on the one-year anniversary of Susie's death?**
   A. Abigail Salmon
   B. Ray Singh
   C. No one knows
   D. Ruth Connors

4. **Where is the first place Abigail goes when she leaves her family?**
   A. A winery in California
   B. Her mother's place
   C. A bar
   D. Her father's cabin in New Hampshire

5. **How does Lindsey know that her mother had an affair with Len Fenerman?**
   A. Her mother tells her
   B. She can just tell
   C. She sees her mother's scarf on Len's desk
   D. Len tells her

6. **Eventually Len fills in all of the blank backs of the photos in his wallet. What does he write?**
   A. The person's name
   B. The date the person died
   C. Dead
   D. Gone

7. **Who are the only three characters allowed in Buckley's fort?**
   A. Samuel, Hal and Holiday
   B. Lindsey, Samuel and Hal
   C. Samuel, Nate and Lindsey
   D. Hal, Nate and Holiday

8. **When Abigail first gets to California, what does she see on the beach that worries her?**
   A. Litter
   B. The waves
   C. The cliffs
   D. A baby sitting alone

9. **Who finds Susie's Pennsylvania keystone charm?**
   A. A hunter
   B. Her father
   C. The police
   D. Len Fenerman

10. **When Ray goes to college, he accidentally finds Susie's picture again. What feature does he focus on?**
    A. Her hair
    B. Her eyes
    C. Her lips
    D. Her rosy cheeks

11. **During the course of the novel, which character does Susie see in heaven after he/she dies?**
    A. George Harvey
    B. Holiday
    C. Ruth
    D. Grandma Lynn

12. **What makes Jack fall back in love with Abigail after she leaves?**
    A. Sorting through the things she left
    B. Looking at pictures Susie took of her
    C. Reading her books
    D. Seeing their children every day

13. **How do Lindsey and Samuel get home after their college graduation?**
    A. They jog
    B. They take Samuel's motorcycle
    C. Jack drives them
    D. Hal picks them up

14. **After Lindsey and Samuel's graduation, which of the following characters sees an image of Susie:**
    A. Buckley
    B. Lindsey
    C. Jack
    D. Lynn

15. **What is Ruth's favorite thing to do while she lives in New York City?**
    A. Take aimless walks in the city
    B. Look for places where women have been killed
    C. Hang out with her friends
    D. Work at a bar

16. **Near the end of the novel, why does Ruth go home for a visit?**
    A. She is due for a visit with her family
    B. Devlopers are going to close up the sinkhole
    C. She needs to solve Susie's murder
    D. She wants to see Ray

17. **What does Buckley plant in the garden?**
    A. Vegetables and herbs
    B. Flowers
    C. Vegetables, herbs and flowers
    D. Herbs

18. **What are Buckley and his father arguing about when his father has a heart attack?**
    A. Why Abigail left
    B. Why Buckley cannot use Susie's clothes for his garden
    C. What Buckley should plant in his garden
    D. How Buckley should have planted more tomatoes

19. **What does Buckley miss the most when his father is not there at night?**
    A. The stories his father tells him before bed
    B. The way his father tucks him in
    C. His father's good night hug
    D. He does not miss his father

20. **When Susie reunites with her grandfather in heaven for the first time, what do they do?**
    A. Dance in silence
    B. Dance to a song her grandfather loves
    C. Watch their family on Earth together
    D. Listen to a song her grandfather loves

21. **What draws Abigail back to her home?**
    A. She misses her children
    B. Jack's heart attack
    C. She feels like a bad mother
    D. She sees Susie everywhere

22. **Where does Abigail leave her photograph of Susie?**
    A. At the airport
    B. In the trash
    C. In her wallet
    D. In California

23. **Who does Abigail get a hold of first when she gets the message that there is an emergecy?**
    A. Buckley
    B. Ruana Singh
    C. The nurse at the hospital
    D. Grandma Lynn

24. **What does Abigail think about when she is sitting on the plane with two empty seats on either sides?**
    A. She is glad the seats are empty so she has privacy
    B. She is glad she does not have a child on either side
    C. She wonders why the flight is so empty
    D. If she were traveling as a mother, she would have a child on each side

25. **75. When Abigail sees Buckley for the first time in many years, who does he remind her of?**
     A. Susie at that age
     B. Jack
     C. Herself when she was 12 and chubby
     D. Jack's father

Quiz 3 Answer Key

1. **(B)** He is too absorbed in his work
2. **(B)** She says she is done with that
3. **(C)** No one knows
4. **(D)** Her father's cabin in New Hampshire
5. **(C)** She sees her mother's scarf on Len's desk
6. **(D)** Gone
7. **(D)** Hal, Nate and Holiday
8. **(D)** A baby sitting alone
9. **(A)** A hunter
10. **(C)** Her lips
11. **(B)** Holiday
12. **(B)** Looking at pictures Susie took of her
13. **(A)** They jog
14. **(A)** Buckley
15. **(B)** Look for places where women have been killed
16. **(B)** Devlopers are going to close up the sinkhole
17. **(C)** Vegetables, herbs and flowers
18. **(B)** Why Buckley cannot use Susie's clothes for his garden
19. **(B)** The way his father tucks him in
20. **(B)** Dance to a song her grandfather loves
21. **(B)** Jack's heart attack
22. **(A)** At the airport
23. **(B)** Ruana Singh
24. **(D)** If she were traveling as a mother, she would have a child on each side
25. **(C)** Herself when she was 12 and chubby

Quiz 4

1. **What does Len fenerman want to give to Jack Salmon when he hears about the heart attack?**
   A. The jingle bell hat that was Susie's
   B. Susie's Pennsylvania keystone charm
   C. An apology for sleeping with his wife
   D. The news that George Harvey has been linked to other murders

2. **What is Jack's nickname for Abigail?**
   A. My little frog
   B. Abb
   C. Ocean Eyes
   D. Gail

3. **What does Abigail order at the diner across from the hospital?**
   A. Meatloaf
   B. Macaroni and cheese
   C. Chicken-fried steak
   D. Coffee

4. **What flower is "Susie's flower"?**
   A. Daffodils
   B. Marigolds
   C. Dandelions
   D. Yellow roses

5. **What does Susie wish more than anything?**
   A. That she could kiss Ray Singh again
   B. That she could be with her family in heaven
   C. That she could get revenge on Mr. Harvey
   D. That she could be with her family one last time

6. **In describing the sinkhole, the newspaper article Ruth has indicates the sinkhole has which of the following human features?**
   A. A mouth
   B. A throat
   C. A stomach
   D. Lips

7. **When Ruth and Ray go to the sinkhole, Ruth sees Susie. What does Ruth ask her?**
    A. "Why are you here?"
    B. "Don't you want anything?"
    C. "Who murdered you?"
    D. "Where is your body?"

8. **When Susie sees George Harvey driving through her neighborhood, who is she worried he might hurt?**
    A. Himself
    B. Lindsey
    C. Ruth
    D. The kids who live in his old house

9. **Near the end of the novel, Susie inhabits Ruth's body. When Ray asks her where she wants to go, what does she say?**
    A. To find Mr. Harvey
    B. To Hal Heckler's bike shop
    C. To her house
    D. To the hospital to see her father

10. **When Susie is about to leave Ruth's body, what does she say to Ray?**
    A. "Thank you"
    B. "I love you"
    C. "You have to read Ruth's journals"
    D. "I'll miss you"

11. **What prompts Ruana to acknowledge that she needs a divorce from her husband?**
    A. She finds out he has been unfaithful
    B. Seeing Ruth and Ray curled up together
    C. Realizing he never eats her apple pies
    D. She hasn't seen him in days

12. **What do Hal and Samuel give to Buckley as an early birthday present?**
    A. A drum set
    B. Gardening tools
    C. A saxophone
    D. A bike

13. **How does Susie describe Ruth Connors?**
    A. Absurd
    B. Cynical
    C. Haunted
    D. Calm

14. **Before Jack and the family arrive home from the hospital, what does Lynn see outside of the kitchen window?**
    A. A garden growing up rapidly
    B. A neighbor's dog
    C. Mr. Harvey driving by the house
    D. A girl sitting in front of Buckley's fort

15. **How do Samuel and Lindsey find out who owns the house they found on Route 30?**
    A. Ruth tells them
    B. They find out from the newspaper
    C. Jack knows the owner personally
    D. Ray Singh tells them

16. **What does Lindsey choose as her profession?**
    A. Forensic scientist
    B. Artist
    C. Therapist
    D. Stay- at home mother

17. **How does Mr. Harvey die?**
    A. He is caught and dies in prison
    B. He is knocked into a ravine by a falling icicle
    C. He dies quietly of a heart attack
    D. He is killed by one of his almost victims

18. **What do Samuel and Lindsey name their daughter?**
    A. Abigail Suzanne
    B. Suzanne Abigail
    C. Susan Lynn
    D. Abigail Lynn

19. **Who does Susie spend time with in "wide wide heaven"?**
    A. Franny
    B. Her grandfather
    C. Grandma Lynn
    D. Holly

20. **What does Mr. Harvey dream about when he feels threatened?**
    A. Susie's scream in the hole in the cornfield
    B. The victim that he let escape
    C. Lindsey as she ran away from his house
    D. The look Susie's father gave him

21. **Why is it important to Susie to be able to leave her family for a new part of heaven?**
    A. So she can stop being so sad for them
    B. So they can forget her
    C. So she can go to a better heaven
    D. So they can move on

22. **What color are Ray Singh's eyes?**
    A. Blue
    B. Gray
    C. Hazel
    D. Brown

23. **When Lindsey and Abigail are getting out of the car after bringing Jack home, who does Abigail tell Lindsey she looks like?**
    A. A younger version of Abigail
    B. Lindsey's father's mother
    C. Grandma Lynn
    D. Susie

24. **Which piece did Susie used to use to play monopoly?**
    A. The hat
    B. The boat
    C. The shoe
    D. The car

25. What does the title Lovely Bones refer to?

    A. The bones of all of Susie's living loved ones

    B. The bones of all of Mr. Harvey's victims

    C. The connections that formed after Susie died

    D. Susie's bones

Quiz 4 Answer Key

1. (**B**) Susie's Pennsylvania keystone charm
2. (**C**) Ocean Eyes
3. (**C**) Chicken-fried steak
4. (**A**) Daffodils
5. (**A**) That she could kiss Ray Singh again
6. (**B**) A throat
7. (**B**) "Don't you want anything?"
8. (**B**) Lindsey
9. (**B**) To Hal Heckler's bike shop
10. (**C**) "You have to read Ruth's journals"
11. (**B**) Seeing Ruth and Ray curled up together
12. (**A**) A drum set
13. (**C**) Haunted
14. (**D**) A girl sitting in front of Buckley's fort
15. (**D**) Ray Singh tells them
16. (**C**) Therapist
17. (**B**) He is knocked into a ravine by a falling icicle
18. (**A**) Abigail Suzanne
19. (**B**) Her grandfather
20. (**C**) Lindsey as she ran away from his house
21. (**D**) So they can move on
22. (**B**) Gray
23. (**B**) Lindsey's father's mother
24. (**C**) The shoe
25. (**C**) The connections that formed after Susie died

ClassicNotes

GradeSaver™

Getting you the grade since 1999™

Other ClassicNotes from GradeSaver™

1984
Absalom, Absalom
Adam Bede
The Adventures of Augie
  March
The Adventures of
  Huckleberry Finn
The Adventures of Tom
  Sawyer
The Aeneid
Agamemnon
The Age of Innocence
The Alchemist (Coelho)
The Alchemist (Jonson)
Alice in Wonderland
All My Sons
All Quiet on the Western
  Front
All the King's Men
All the Pretty Horses
Allen Ginsberg's Poetry
The Ambassadors
American Beauty
And Then There Were
  None
Angela's Ashes
Animal Farm
Anna Karenina
Anthem
Antigone
Antony and Cleopatra
Aristotle's Ethics
Aristotle's Poetics
Aristotle's Politics
As I Lay Dying
As You Like It

Astrophil and Stella
Atlas Shrugged
Atonement
The Awakening
Babbitt
The Bacchae
Bartleby the Scrivener
The Bean Trees
The Bell Jar
Beloved
Benito Cereno
Beowulf
Bhagavad-Gita
Billy Budd
Black Boy
Bleak House
Bless Me, Ultima
Blindness
The Bloody Chamber
Bluest Eye
The Bonfire of the
  Vanities
The Book of the Duchess
  and Other Poems
The Book Thief
Brave New World
Breakfast at Tiffany's
Breakfast of Champions
The Brief Wondrous Life
  of Oscar Wao
The Brothers Karamazov
The Burning Plain and
  Other Stories
A Burnt-Out Case
By Night in Chile
Call of the Wild

Candide
The Canterbury Tales
Cat on a Hot Tin Roof
Cat's Cradle
Catch-22
The Catcher in the Rye
The Caucasian Chalk
  Circle
Charlotte's Web
The Cherry Orchard
The Chocolate War
The Chosen
A Christmas Carol
Christopher Marlowe's
  Poems
Chronicle of a Death
  Foretold
Civil Disobedience
Civilization and Its
  Discontents
A Clockwork Orange
The Color of Water
The Color Purple
Comedy of Errors
Communist Manifesto
A Confederacy of
  Dunces
Confessions
Connecticut Yankee in
  King Arthur's Court
The Consolation of
  Philosophy
Coriolanus
The Count of Monte
  Cristo
The Country Wife

For our full list of over 250 Study Guides, Quizzes,
Sample College Application Essays, Literature Essays and E-texts, visit:

www.gradesaver.com

ClassicNotes

GradeSaver™

Getting you the grade since 1999™

Other ClassicNotes from GradeSaver™

Into the Wild
Invisible Man
The Island of Dr. Moreau
Jane Eyre
Jazz
The Jew of Malta
Joseph Andrews
The Joy Luck Club
Julius Caesar
The Jungle
Jungle of Cities
Kama Sutra
Kate Chopin's Short
   Stories
Kidnapped
King Lear
The Kite Runner
Last of the Mohicans
Leaves of Grass
The Legend of Sleepy
   Hollow
Leviathan
Libation Bearers
Life is Beautiful
Life of Pi
Light In August
The Lion, the Witch and
   the Wardrobe
Little Women
Lolita
Long Day's Journey Into
   Night
Look Back in Anger
Lord Jim
Lord of the Flies

The Lord of the Rings:
   The Fellowship of the
   Ring
The Lord of the Rings:
   The Return of the
   King
The Lord of the Rings:
   The Two Towers
A Lost Lady
The Lottery and Other
   Stories
Love in the Time of
   Cholera
The Love Song of J.
   Alfred Prufrock
The Lovely Bones
Lucy
Macbeth
Madame Bovary
Maggie: A Girl of the
   Streets and Other
   Stories
Manhattan Transfer
Mankind: Medieval
   Morality Plays
Mansfield Park
The Master and
   Margarita
MAUS
The Mayor of
   Casterbridge
Measure for Measure
Medea
Merchant of Venice
Metamorphoses
The Metamorphosis

Middlemarch
A Midsummer Night's
   Dream
Moby Dick
A Modest Proposal and
   Other Satires
Moll Flanders
Mother Courage and Her
   Children
Mrs. Dalloway
Much Ado About
   Nothing
My Antonia
Mythology
Native Son
Nickel and Dimed: On
   (Not) Getting By in
   America
Night
Nine Stories
No Exit
Northanger Abbey
Notes from Underground
O Pioneers
The Odyssey
Oedipus Rex or Oedipus
   the King
Of Mice and Men
The Old Man and the Sea
Oliver Twist
On Liberty
On the Road
One Day in the Life of
   Ivan Denisovich
One Flew Over the
   Cuckoo's Nest

For our full list of over 250 Study Guides, Quizzes,
Sample College Application Essays, Literature Essays and E-texts, visit:

www.gradesaver.com

ClassicNotes

GradeSaver™

Getting you the grade since 1999™

For our full list of over 250 Study Guides, Quizzes,
Sample College Application Essays, Literature Essays and E-texts, visit:

www.gradesaver.com

Made in the USA
Lexington, KY
15 August 2011